# Two Spanish Verse Chap-books

T0371435

# TWO SPANISH VERSE CHAP-BOOKS

ROMANÇE DE AMADIS (*c. 1515–19*)
JUYZIO HALLADO Y TROBADO (*c. 1510*)

## A FACSIMILE EDITION
### WITH BIBLIOGRAPHICAL AND TEXTUAL STUDIES

BY

F. J. NORTON

*Under-Librarian, University Library, Cambridge, and*
*Fellow of University College*

AND

EDWARD M. WILSON, F.B.A.

*Professor of Spanish in the University of Cambridge, and*
*Fellow of Emmanuel College*

CAMBRIDGE
AT THE UNIVERSITY PRESS
1969

CAMBRIDGE UNIVERSITY PRESS
Cambridge, New York, Melbourne, Madrid, Cape Town, Singapore,
São Paulo, Delhi, Dubai, Tokyo

Cambridge University Press
The Edinburgh Building, Cambridge CB2 8RU, UK

Published in the United States of America by Cambridge University Press, New York

www.cambridge.org
Information on this title: www.cambridge.org/9780521134941

© Cambridge University Press 1969

This publication is in copyright. Subject to statutory exception
and to the provisions of relevant collective licensing agreements,
no reproduction of any part may take place without the written
permission of Cambridge University Press.

First published 1969
This digitally printed version 2010

*A catalogue record for this publication is available from the British Library*

*Library of Congress Catalogue Card Number: 68-8345*

ISBN 978-0-521-05843-8 Hardback
ISBN 978-0-521-13494-1 Paperback

Cambridge University Press has no responsibility for the persistence or
accuracy of URLs for external or third-party internet websites referred to in
this publication, and does not guarantee that any content on such websites is,
or will remain, accurate or appropriate.

*To*

ANTONIO RODRÍGUEZ-MOÑINO

# Contents

# *Preface*

Norton wrote chapters I to IV; Wilson wrote V to VII. Norton also supplied details of places, printers and dates of imprintless undated chap-books mentioned in chapters V and VII.

Some readers may consider our use of the word chap-book anachronistic. Our use of this relatively modern term is deliberate. The Spanish *pliegos sueltos* need an English equivalent, and chap-book is the best one. They are not broadsheets; they are folded and printed on both sides of the paper. They were sold by chapmen and by blind beggars.

We thank the University Librarian (Mr H. R. Creswick) and the Syndics of the Cambridge University Library for their permission to make this book. We thank Don Antonio Rodríguez-Moñino for his invaluable help during many years' friendship and particularly for his communication of the existence of the chap-books at Vienna. We thank Professor Kenneth H. Jackson, F.B.A., for permission to quote from his Rede Lecture for 1964, and Dr Peter Rickard both for his help with French parallels in chapters V and VII and for his criticism of the typescript of the last three chapters. Our debts to other scholars are mentioned in our notes, but we wish also to pay tribute to the works of an older generation who chiefly made our work possible: Don Ramón Menéndez Pidal, the late Sir Henry Thomas and the late Professor William J. Entwistle.

# Abbreviated References

*Cancionero de Amberes*
*Cancionero de romances impresos en Amberes sin año.* Edición facsímil con una introducción por R. Menéndez Pidal, nueva ed., Madrid, 1945.

Durán
*Romancero general, ó coleccion de romances castellanos anteriores al siglo XVIII. Recogidos...por* Agustin Duran, Biblioteca de Autores Españoles, x & xvi.

Entwistle
William J. Entwistle, *European balladry*, Oxford, 1951.

Norton
F. J. Norton, *Printing in Spain, 1501–1520*, Cambridge, 1966.

*Pliegos*, Madrid
*Pliegos poéticos góticos de la Biblioteca Nacional*, 6 vols, Madrid, 1957–61.

*Pliegos*, Morbecq
Antonio Rodríguez-Moñino, *Los pliegos poéticos de la colección del Marqués de Morbecq (siglo XVI).* Edición en facsímile, precedida de un estudio bibliográfico, Madrid, 1962.

*Pliegos*, Praga
*Pliegos poéticos españoles en la Universidad de Praga*, 2 vols, Madrid, 1960.

*Romancero hispánico*
R. Menéndez Pidal, *Romancero hispánico*, 2 vols, Madrid, 1953.

Thomas, *Early*
*Early Spanish ballads in the British Museum.* Edited...by Henry Thomas, 3 vols, Cambridge, 1927. (1, *Romance del conde Dirlos*, printed by G. Coci Saragossa *c.* 1510. 2, *Romance del conde Alarcos*, printed by G. Coci Saragossa *c.* 1520. 3, *Romance de don Gayferos*, printed by J. Cromberger, Seville, *c.* 1515.)

Thomas, *Thirteen*
*Thirteen Spanish ballads printed in Burgos 1516–17 now in the British Museum.* Edited by Henry Thomas, Barcelona, 1931.

Wolf & Hofmann
*Primavera y flor de romances...* Publicada por F. J. Wolf y C. Hofmann, 2 vols, Berlin, 1856.

# CHAPTER I

## History of the Volume

THE two works now reproduced constitute a slender volume bound in brown morocco by Koehler and bearing a leather label inscribed 'Ex Musæo Caroli Nodier'. The titles of the two pieces are, in fact, transcribed at no. 690 of Nodier's catalogue, compiled for his own purposes but only printed in time to serve as the catalogue of the sale of his books after his death in January 1844.[1] Nodier's description does not attempt to date the two works or to identify their places of printing, but ends with a note which shows that they were acquired at a Thorpe sale from among a greater number appearing to derive from a collective volume which had been broken up.[2] A marked copy of the catalogue shows that no. 690 was sold for 81 francs. From that time Nodier's volume seems to have remained in private hands, unnoticed except for a brief extract from his catalogue relating to the *Romançe de Amadis* in Palau's *Manual*, until a few years ago when it was acquired by M. Georges Heilbrun, of Paris, from whose catalogue it was purchased for the Cambridge University Library in the spring of 1964.[3]

No other copies of these two chap-books have been traced.

[1] *Description raisonnée d'une jolie collection de livres (nouveaux mélanges tirés d'une petite bibliothèque), par Charles Nodier*, Paris, 1844.

[2] 'Il y a peu de livrets plus rares que ces vieilles pièces de poésie espagnole en éditions originales. Une vente de Thorp en offrit certains nombres qui paroissoient avoir été détachées d'un recueil peut-être unique. Obligé de me borner, je m'arrêtai à celles-ci, les mieux conservées de toutes, et parmi lesquelles se trouve la fameuse romance de Gayferos, à jamais célèbre par un des chapitres les plus piquants de *Don Quichotte*. Une collection complète et *princeps* de ces chants du *Romancero* vaudroit la rançon d'un roi, et je connois un homme qui ne l'échangeroit pas contre la grandesse.' The following entry may be relevant: 'ROMANCES, a curious collection of Single Romances in the Spanish language, *woodcuts*' at no. 75 on p. 4 of *Catalogue of splendid, curious, and valuable books, selected from the stock of Mr. Thorpe... which...will be sold by auction, by Mr. Evans, at his house, No. 93, Pall Mall, on Wednesday, April 5, and three following days.* 1826.

[3] *Éditions originales du XVe au XXe siècle provenant en partie des bibliothèques de deux amateurs.* Georges Heilbrun, Paris (1964), no. 310.

# CHAPTER II

# *The Printers*

### (i) *Romançe de Amadis*

THE material, both types and woodcut, may be identified with certainty as belonging to the press founded at Burgos before March 1485 by Fadrique de Basilea, that is Friedrich of Basel, who, though he is not known to have used his surname in Spain, was in all probability the Friedrich Biel who was printing in association with Michael Wenssler at Basel, *c.* 1472. Fadrique's latest surviving dated work is the *Flor de virtudes* of 22 August 1517. By 1518 his press had passed to Alonso de Melgar, whose earliest signed work is of 28 August 1518, although unsigned works with the Burgos imprint of 14 April and 16 August 1518 may also be fairly attributed to him. Melgar is known to have been married to Fadrique's daughter Isabel. His tenure of the press was brief. He was still printing in September 1525, but a book of the following January was issued in the name of his widow; from 1527 the signed production of the press bore the name of Juan de Junta, who is known from documentary evidence to have married Melgar's widow.[1]

Three gothic founts are used in the book. The large heading-type of the first line of the title is first found in use by Fadrique in his *Manuale Burgense* of 1508. It was employed regularly by Melgar but found little favour with Junta who at once replaced it with a fount which had made its appearance in Seville many years earlier, though he was later to make occasional use of the rejected material. The smaller heading-type, used only on the verso of leaf 4, had been introduced by Fadrique in 1498 and continued to be used by his successors. The text-type, measuring 97 mm. for 20 lines, is first found in use by Fadrique in 1490; in the summer of 1515 it appears to have been recast, a permanent change[2] being made in the form of the

---

[1] For the marriages of Isabel de Basilea see Luisa Cuesta Gutiérrez, *La imprenta en Salamanca* (Salamanca, 1960), pp. 27 and 58.

[2] This change was first noted by Sir Henry Thomas (introduction to Thomas, *Thirteen*). The time of the change, given as between April 1515 and February 1516, may now be more closely defined; the modified d is already found in the *Intonationes* of Gonzalo Martínez de Biscargui, of 15 September 1515 (copy in Biblioteca Nacional, Lisbon).

lower-case d, whose top, previously inclined, was henceforth almost horizontal. The modified type remained in use by Melgar, but perhaps for no more than the first year of his activity, its last fully dated occurrence being in the *Flosculus sacramentorum* of Pedro Fernández de Villegas, of 30 September 1518. His next dated work, the *Remedio de jugadores* of Pedro de Covarrubias, of 24 November 1519, shows an entirely different gothic text-type, one which had been introduced at Logroño in 1517 by Arnao Guillén de Brocar, a printer with whom both Fadrique and Melgar had close relations, for they printed a number of books on his behalf. By 1524 (in the *Farsa del mundo* of López de Yanguas, for example) Melgar was adulterating his new type with a considerable admixture of capitals from its predecessor; this impure form was continued by Juan de Junta, and is found in various chap-books printed by him. Eventually Junta was to make some use of a purer form of Fadrique's fount, differing only in its retention of the semi-circular paragraph-mark from Melgar's fount of 1519 in the place of Fadrique's characteristic tailed form. The latter was virtually abandoned after 1518; I have noticed but two isolated later appearances in a considerable number of relevant chap-books examined, and the fact that the remaining paragraph-marks (40 in one case, 37 in the other) in the tracts concerned are of the later form shows that its use was inadvertent.[1]

The *Romançe de Amadis* shows the modified d in its text-type and consistently uses Fadrique's tailed paragraph-mark. It must therefore have been printed after April 1515 and before November 1519, either by Fadrique de Basilea or by Alonso de Melgar.[2] It is by no means impossible that the printing of the group of nine chap-books to which it belongs was begun by Fadrique and continued by Melgar.

The woodcut beneath the title was printed from a block cut to illustrate Act XII of the *Comedia de Calisto y Melibea*, the earliest surviving edition of the *Celestina*, printed by Fadrique de Basilea *c.* 1499. This block was still in use, though by now sadly deteriorated, in several chap-books printed at Burgos in the middle of the century or later.

---

[1] The chap-books concerned are reproduced in *Pliegos*, Praga, II, lxxv, and *Pliegos*, Madrid, II, lxi, respectively. Both may be later works by Melgar rather than by Junta.

[2] The same dating and attribution must apply to the two ballad-books in the British Museum reprinted in Thomas, *Thirteen*.

## (ii) *Juyzio hallado y trobado*

A detailed examination of its types reveals that the *Juyzio* was printed at Salamanca by Juan de Porras. The heading-type (153 mm.) was introduced, in an earlier state, in 1496 by the anonymous Salamanca press which passed into his hands at a date as yet unknown. His first signed colophon is of 1502, but since he put his name to his numerous subsequent works only sparingly—his next signature is of 1506—it is likely enough that he came into possession of the anonymous press at an earlier, perhaps a much earlier, date. It is known that he was established in the city as a bookseller in 1491. From 1502 the heading-type here used is found only in books printed by Porras. The text-type (92 mm.) is one of those most widely used in Spain in the early sixteenth century. It is of Parisian design and was introduced at Pamplona in 1499 by Arnao Guillén de Brocar. With only the slightest modifications it was adopted in the next few years by several other printers, including Hagembach's anonymous successor at Toledo, Juan Varela, Jacobo Cromberger and Porras. As here used the type conforms in all its details to that owned by Porras. It is first found in the original edition of the *Leyes de Toro* printed by him anonymously—or strictly speaking in the name of one Pedro de Pascua, presumably a bookseller or merchant—probably in 1505. He subsequently made but little use of it and, in its pure state, appears to have abandoned it altogether after he had printed, again anonymously, Juan Remón de Trasmiera's *Triumpho Raymundino* at a date which was probably very close to 1512. Thereafter he preferred to use a very different fount of the same size which had been introduced by the anonymous press as early as 1492, though he occasionally employed a typographical hybrid compounded of elements from both founts as well as from a third which is not to be found isolated. The line 'que enel quinientos y dos' (folio 3 verso, col. 2) suggests that the date of composition may have been 1501; the types show that printing took place in the period 1505–12, and *c.* 1510 may be advanced as a round date. No other chap-book printed by Porras is known.

A copy of this work, probably though not demonstrably of this edition, was in the possession of Fernando Colón, whose manuscript *Abecedarium* records both its title and the first line of its text (no. 15162).

# CHAPTER III

# The Poetical Chap-book in Spain up to 1520

THE *Romançe de Amadis* is a typical example of the Spanish sixteenth-century poetical chap-book, both in its literary content, which is a miscellany of poems, in this instance *romances*, and in its physical aspects—its quarto format, the restriction of its text to a single folded sheet, its title embellished by an irrelevant reused woodcut with the text beginning immediately below in two columns, its gothic types, and its lack of any indication of place, printer or date.

The poetical chap-book was not a set form to which the early printers deliberately conformed, and many examples are to be found which are far from possessing all the above characteristics. The text may be partly in prose as in *Cartas y coplas para requerir nueuos amores*, of which the earliest editions known were printed anonymously at Toledo by Juan de Villaquirán (*c.* 1515?), and at Seville by Jacobo Cromberger (*c.* 1516–20); there are marginal cases in which verse is merely used to fill out space left over at the end of a prose chap-book, as in a *Pronostico* by Fray Diego de Torres for the years 1520–5, printed in the types of Jorge Costilla of Valencia, whose last page is occupied by a *Romance del nacimiento de nuestro señor*, the unacknowledged work of Torres Naharro.[1] Some texts are versified accounts of current events and other matters of public interest; many of these are known only from the manuscript catalogues of Fernando Colón: the survivors include *Coplas hechas sobre vn caso acontescido en Xerez de la frontera de vn hombre que mato veynte y dos personas a traycion* (Cromberger, *c.* 1515?), and *Elegia: fecha ala muerte del catholico rey don Fernando de gloriosa memoria. Enla qual se haze mencion delo mas substancial de su testamento* (Seville, Juan Varela, 1516?). There is a long series of chap-books containing devotional poetry, much of it by named or known authors; perhaps the earliest is *Coplas hechas por fray ambrosio montesino dela coluna del señor* (*c.* 1510?), a reprint from the author's *Cancionero de diuersas obras* (Toledo, 1508), and the work of the same anonymous

---

[1] For fuller details of the chap-books mentioned in this section see the *List of poetical chap-books up to 1520* (referred to as *List*).

5

press. The text of the secular chap-books may be restricted to a single work—an eclogue, a long *romance* such as *Don Gayferos*, or a long poem by such a popular author as Rodrigo de Reynosa—but is more usually a miscellany like the *Romançe de Amadis*. Its matter may derive from printed sources or, as far as can be ascertained, make its first appearance in chap-book form. Perhaps the only factor common to all these works is that they were cheap editions intended for the man in the street but, even so, while some could suitably be read or sung to the illiterate, others, such as the poems of Garcisánchez de Badajoz, demanded a certain sophistication in their audience.[1] The language of this material is invariably Castilian and it is regrettable that very little can be said of its counterparts in Catalan. Except for three or four devotional pieces printed in Valencia and Barcelona which approximate to the type none has survived, but that they once existed is demonstrated by the catalogues of Fernando Colón. Among others he possessed a copy of the *Cobles de les tres naus de conserva*, bought by him in Tarragona in 1513 for one *diner* (*Regestrum* 3970); it was doubtless printed in Barcelona, where it was reprinted as a quarto of two leaves in 1596.

The physical aspects of the poetical chap-books are equally variable. At Seville the folio form was used, perhaps experimentally, by Jacobo Cromberger for a *Romance nueuamente hecho de Calisto y Melibea*, whose printing and ornamental material can be assigned to *c.* 1513, and for a *Romance de don gayferos*, doubtless of the same time; these folio pieces are also exceptional in being printed in four and three columns respectively. While a single gathering is universal in the early period its extent may vary considerably; four leaves is normal, but two not infrequent, and gatherings of six or twelve leaves are not exceptional. Unillustrated chap-books are quite common; in the period 1511–15 Cromberger printed both an illustrated and an unillustrated quarto edition of the *Romance de don gayferos*. Some chap-books from Seville and Toledo have full title-pages with woodcut borders. The one strictly constant feature of the lay-out is the complete absence of any printer's colophon.

[1] The *Regestrum* of Fernando Colón usually records the price he paid for each item. A selection of his entries for Spanish verse chap-books may be conveniently consulted in Don Antonio Rodríguez-Moñino's *Doscientos pliegos poéticos desconocidos, anteriores a 1540; noticias bibliográficas*, México, 1961 (reprinted from *Nueva Revista de Filología Hispánica*, XV (1961), 81–106); this also includes transcripts from Colón's *Abecedarium*, which gives no prices. For a copy of *Dos romances del marques de Mantua* (*Regestrum* 4043) Colón paid four maravedís at Medina del Campo in 1524. This was either the quarto of twelve leaves printed in the types of Arnao Guillén de Brocar, very likely at his Valladolid press, *c.* 1515–19, or an edition corresponding very closely to it. Brocar's edition is the one known poetical chap-book printed by him.

Since it is reasonably certain that more of these early editions have perished without trace than have survived, or even been recorded, it is not possible to trace the earliest stages of their development with any confidence. It may be said however that the oldest known examples fall into the category of the versified narration of contemporary events, and it is at least conceivable that it was their commercial success that turned the attention of the printers and booksellers to the fuller possibilities of the popular market. The works concerned are the *Coplas fechas alos altos estados delos reys nuestros señores*, referring to a Valladolid ceremony of the early summer of 1496 in connection with the impending marriage of the Infanta Juana, and the *Coplas fechas sobre el casamiento dela hija del Rey despaña conel hijo del emperador*, a narration of the departure of the Infanta in August 1496 for her marriage to the Archduke Philip and of her arrival in Flanders. Neither work has a colophon, but the first is in the types of the Burgos printer Juan de Burgos and the second in those of Fadrique de Basilea. The printing doubtless followed close upon the events described. Both tracts are quartos of four leaves printed in two columns, the first with an illustrated title-page, the second with the text following a title of page width and concluding with two woodcuts. In the Escorial Library there is another anonymous poetical pamphlet in Fadrique's types and probably of the closing years of the same decade. Although it does not lack popular characteristics, its intention, conceivably instructional, is not clear, and its lay-out does not suggest that it forms a true link in our chain. It is a quarto of eight leaves beginning with a poem whose title, at the head of the first column, is *Siguen se vnas Coplas muy deuotas fechas a reuerencia del nacimiento de nuestro señor jesu cristo*. Its second poem, printed in long lines, is headed by a detailed note of its metre and is followed by an enigmatic final note, 'Comparacion de nombre. Guis sin par, es el vuestro nombre, añadiendo el tercero hombre'.[1]

The next surviving book, *Coplas fechas por mandado de vn señor el qual tenia vn moço adeuino*, is the first to conform closely to the strict pattern of the poetical chap-book as exemplified by the *Romançe de Amadis*. It is yet another anonymous production of Fadrique's press. Unfortunately it is not possible to date it closely on typographical grounds since its types were in use unchanged for some years before and after 1500, but its rather more fully developed lay-out suggests that it should be placed somewhat later than Fadrique's *Coplas sobre el casamiento* and possibly *c.* 1500–5. In addition to

[1] This description is based on the reproductions in F. Vindel's *El arte tipográfico en España durante el siglo XV*. *Burgos y Guadalajara* (Madrid, 1951), pp. 271–3. The *Gesamtkatalog's* description (no. 7466) is incomplete.

the jocose title-poem it contains two equally anonymous poems of an amatory character. Except that it has no woodcut its physical characteristics are those of the *Romançe de Amadis*.

An *Egloga interlocutoria: graciosa y por gentil estilo nueuamente trobada por diego de auila* can hardly be described as a chap-book since it has the collation $a^8b^8c^2$; moreover it has a colophon—'Emprimiose en alcala de henares'.[1] On the other hand its closing pages are occupied in true chap-book fashion by an unrelated work, *Vnas coplas pastoriles para cantar*, by Rodrigo de Reynosa. The book is in the characteristic types of Stanislao Polono, whose activity at Alcalá was limited to the years 1502–4. With the exception of a prose *Carta dela gran victoria y presa de Oran*, a tract of two leaves partly occupied by indifferent verses on the same subject and printed in the types of Carles Amoros of Barcelona, doubtless in 1509, the remaining manifestations of verse chap-book printing attributable to the first decade of the century are confined to the presses of the anonymous successor to Pedro Hagembach at Toledo and of Jorge Coci at Saragossa. A devotional poem of *c*. 1510 by Ambrosio Montesino from the Toledo press has already been mentioned. The *Razonamiento por coplas en que se contrahaze la jermania y fieros de los rufianes y las mugeres del partido...Fechas por rodrigo de reynosa* may well be a little earlier (*c*. 1505–10) in view of the character of its bordered title-page, which is typical of Toledo work of the decade. The *Romance del conde Dirlos* in the types of Jorge Coci was well dated by Sir Henry Thomas at *c*. 1510; it reuses woodcut material made for a book of April 1509.[2] Space on its twelfth and last leaf is utilized for the inclusion of a short devotional poem by Diego de Pegera. The title notes that this edition adds certain things not hitherto included, a clear reference to the existence of at least one earlier edition, now unknown.[3] The added matter was perhaps merely Pegera's piece. The only other works of this class from the earlier years of Coci's press are a *Romance del conde Alarcos* and a *Reprehension de vicios y estados en general conpuesto por vn religioso de obseruancia*, both of *c*. 1520; the *Reprehension* includes other poems of a more secular character.

The number of surviving editions suggests that the poetical chap-book only came into its own in the second decade of the century and from about 1513. This increased

---

[1] *Gallardo* *4540; the copy there described has been lost to sight, but fortunately the first page was reproduced in Pedro Vindel's *Catálogo de una colección de cien obras raras procedentes de la Biblioteca del Excmo Marqués de Laurencín* (Madrid, 1927), no. 8, and repeated in Francisco Vindel's *Manual gráfico-descriptivo* (no. 210).

[2] See Thomas, *Early*, vol. I, p. 9.

[3] For the full title see *List*, 23.

activity appears to have been centred in Seville on the presses of Jacobo Cromberger, who had already printed popular works in prose. His earliest known work in strictly chap-book form is a prose *Iuyzio fecho por francisco diodato astrologo famoso dela cibdad de luca del año de .m.d.xj. y del año de .m.d.xij.*, a quarto of four leaves, the last of which is occupied by a *Iuyzio nueuamente hecho por Pedro de frias hermitaño en roma,* in verse and in double column. The prose prognostication is a translation of a work doubtless published in Italy late in 1510, and presumably appeared in Seville early in 1511. A versified *Testamento dela reyna doña ysabel nueuamente trobado por Ieronimo del enzina*, a quarto of two leaves in Cromberger's types, ends with the same verses by Pedro de Frias and may well have been printed later in the same year. Perhaps the earliest true poetical chap-book from Cromberger's presses is the *Coplas del conde de parades* [*sic*, for *paredes*]... *Y otras coplas de Montoro,* which was possibly printed as early as 1512. The great significance of this little miscellany is that all its texts had appeared in the first edition of the *Cancionero general*, printed in Valencia in 1511. The popularity of this extensive compilation—it reached its fourth edition in 1520—and the opportunity of drawing upon its treasures may well have been the principal stimulus for the sudden blossoming of the poetical chap-book. Although it was protected by royal privilege Cromberger was to make considerable further use of this source, and his example was followed by other printers. The one other collection which was extensively pillaged by the chap-books was the *Cancionero de todas las obras de Juan del Enzina*. It must be emphasized, however, that for much of the poetical material contained in the chap-books, for example a number of the traditional ballad texts and above all the poems of Rodrigo de Reynosa, who is not represented in the *Cancionero general*, no printed source is known. It is even conceivable that some poems from chap-books were in their turn received into the considerably changed second edition of the *Cancionero general* (Valencia, 1514).[1]

Altogether, twenty-five poetical chap-books have been traced which were printed

[1] *Las maldiciones dichas clara escura del mismo garcisanchez de badajoz* (*List,* 34) contains three poems by Garcisánchez, two of them included in the 1511 *Cancionero general*, the third added in 1514. It is printed in Cromberger's types, which show characteristics obtaining only from 1510 to the early months of 1516, and there is no typographical reason why it should not have preceded the 1514 *Cancionero*. The peculiarly worded title is perhaps a careless adjustment of the heading 'Otra obra suya' of the 1511 *Cancionero*; that the chap-book is complete is shown by another printing (*c.* 1515) made at Toledo by Villaquirán, which has exactly the same title. The task of collating chap-book texts with the *Cancionero general* (and with one another) has yet to be accomplished; a solid basis for it is provided by the detailed indexes in Don Antonio Rodríguez-Moñino's admirable *Noticias bibliográficas* prefixed to the Spanish Academy's facsimile (1958) of the 1511 *Cancionero general*.

by Cromberger not later than early 1516, six more lack the tell-tale typographical peculiarities which enable such a dating to be made but probably belong to the same period, and another nine were printed after this typographical date-line but probably before the end of 1520. These forty books of Cromberger's form by far the largest contribution from any Spanish press of the period, but it should be borne in mind that their survival can only be regarded as accidental. With five exceptions Cromberger's editions are to be found only in the national libraries of London, Paris and Vienna. The British Museum's copies were acquired for Grenville by a friend in Spain and perhaps, together with his Burgos chap-books, had formed part of a single collection. The Paris chap-books are all contained in two volumes, apparently unrelated, and the small collection at Vienna possibly comes from a single source. It has already been noted that Brocar's press is represented by one piece only and Coci's by three, all in unique copies; one may suppose that these are chance survivors from a larger output. But for the existence of a tract volume in the public library of Oporto we should not know that a second Seville printer, Juan Varela de Salamanca, also participated in this branch of his trade. The volume includes seven poetical tracts printed by Varela and dating from 1516 to 1519, one of them, *Coplas de Madalenica*, a close reprint from Cromberger's repertory; it also adds five chap-books to the three otherwise known printed at Toledo in the types of Juan de Villaquirán.[1]

Fadrique de Basilea is not known to have produced any immediate successors to the *Coplas fechas por mandado de vn señor* and when we again find him engaged in printing poetical chap-books it may have been in emulation of Cromberger's success rather than in continuation of a personal tradition. The earliest product of this revival is entitled *Aqui comiençan vnas coplas de Iuan agraz*. It is a very clear case of pilfering from the *Cancionero general* of 1511. The seven poems contained in its four leaves are to be found in the same order and consecutively in the *Cancionero general*— one of them is omitted by the 1514 edition. That the borrowing was done by Fadrique is proved by his omission of the next poem in the *Cancionero*, which is a reply, for which he had no room, to his seventh piece. It is demonstrable, on typographical grounds, that the printing was done before mid-September 1515. The Bibliothèque Nationale copy is bound in a volume which includes five more chap-books in Fadrique's types, among them the *Coplas de las comadres* of Rodrigo de

[1] See A. Rodríguez-Moñino, *Pliegos poéticos de Oporto...* (With *Notas tipográficas* by F. J. Norton), Coimbra, 1963 (reprinted from *Arquivo de Bibliografia Portuguesa*, 1963).

Reynosa and the *Romance de la Melisenda hija del emperador,* and all five belong to the same group as the *Romançe de Amadis* and the two British Museum chap-books, that is to say that they can be dated after April 1515 and before November 1519 and some, or even all, of them may be early works of Fadrique's successor Alonso de Melgar. Melgar maintained the tradition of chap-book printing after he had changed his main text-type (by November 1519); a *Pater noster trobabo* [*sic*] by Rodrigo de Reynosa and a *Romance nueuo por muy gentil estilo* show the new type in its short-lived pure form and may be assigned to *c.* 1520. The *Romance nueuo* is contained in a bulky volume preserved at Prague which includes a considerable number of chap-books printed by Melgar's successors Juan and Felipe de Junta, who made Burgos the chief centre of the Spanish chap-book trade for the next fifty years.[1]

A defective copy has survived of a *Romance de los doze pares de Francia* (with other poems) printed in the types of Joan Rosembach of Barcelona in the second decade of the century and quite possibly *c.* 1513.[2] Fernando Colón's *Regestrum* yields tenuous indications that further Castilian works of this class may have been printed in Barcelona in the same decade. In August 1513 he bought at Tarragona for half a *diner* apiece copies of *Coplas de la bella mal maridada* (*Regestrum* 3967) and *Perque de amores* (3966); most of his Tarragona purchases either have the Barcelona imprint or may fairly be conjectured to have been printed in Barcelona. Another of the same group of acquisitions, the *Cancionero de Rodrigo de Reynosa de Coplas de Nuestra Señora* (3950), with a colophon of Barcelona, 1513, must have been a considerably larger work, for it cost six *diners.*

---

[1] All the eighty-one Prague chap-books are reproduced in *Pliegos,* Praga. No. XVI, *Romance de Durandarte,* also has the appearance of being a work by Melgar of *c.* 1520; it uses a smaller text-type (78 mm.) introduced by his predecessor.

[2] See Norton, p. 184, no. 1. The copy has now been located; it is in the custody of Don Gonzalo Menéndez-Pidal Goyri as part of the material for the *Romancero tradicional de las lenguas hispánicas.* I am indebted to Señor Menéndez-Pidal Goyri both for his kindness in allowing me to see the original and for the generous gift of photographs of it. The accompanying fragments of the *Romance del conde Dirlos* prove on examination to be mid-sixteenth-century work.

# CHAPTER IV

## List of Poetical Chap-books up to 1520
### (including marginal works)

EXCEPT for no. 41 the list is restricted to located books. It is intended to be complete, but the universal absence of colophons in books of this class makes it reasonably certain that further works exist which are at present unidentified. For the same reason the only basis for bibliographical identification is a typographical examination; all the books included have either been seen or been investigated through the medium of photographs. All attributions to presses may be regarded as firmly established. Dating is largely based on known changes in the material of the printer concerned, and must necessarily vary in its degree of closeness.

The entries are arranged alphabetically under alphabetically arranged headings for authors or, failing them, for persons, real or imaginary, or for places, named in the title and dealt with in the books or, failing them, for the first noun or adjective of the title, ignoring introductory phrases. Successive editions are arranged chronologically.

Each entry includes:

(1) A transcript of its title, showing line-endings and retaining punctuation, abbreviations and contractions, but not distinguishing the various forms of d, r and s; occasional shortenings are indicated by .... Ornamental initial capitals are enclosed in ( ); index figures following an initial capital indicate its height in terms of lines of text.

(2) A note of format, of collation, of the number of columns per page if other than two, of the existence of a title-page proper, of the location of woodcuts, of the place of printing, printer and suggested date, and of the location of all copies traced. All books are in gothic types, none shows printed foliation.

(3) A transcription of the heading and first line of each component poem.

When the edition is available in a published facsimile or a modern edited text this is indicated in an added note.

ABBREVIATIONS

*Printing places*

| | | |
|---|---|---|
| Alc[alá] | Sal[amanca] | Tol[edo] |
| Bar[celona] | Sar[agossa] | Val[encia] |
| Bur[gos] | Sev[ille] | Vall[adolid] |

*Printers*

| | | | | |
|---|---|---|---|---|
| Amor. | Carles Amorós | | Mel. | Alonso de Melgar |
| Bas. | Fadrique de Basilea | | Porr. | Juan de Porras |
| J. de Bur. | Juan de Burgos | | Ros. | Joan Rosembach |
| Cost. | Jorge Costilla | | Var. | Juan Varela de Salamanca |
| Crom. | Jacobo Cromberger | | Vill. | Juan de Villaquirán |
| Hag. succ. | Successor to Pedro Hagembach | | | |

*Libraries*

| | | | | |
|---|---|---|---|---|
| BM | British Museum | | Norton | F. J. Norton, Cambridge |
| BNM | Biblioteca Nacional, Madrid | | ÖNB | Österreichische Nationalbibliothek, Vienna |
| BNP | Bibliothèque Nationale, Paris | | | |
| LC | Library of Congress, Washington | | Oporto | Biblioteca Pública Municipal, Oporto |
| March | Library of Don Bartolomé March Servera, Madrid (incorporates the former Medina-celi Library) | | Rodríguez-Moñino | Library of Don Antonio Ro-dríguez-Moñino, Madrid |
| | | | Santander | Biblioteca Menéndez y Pelayo, Santander |
| G. Menéndez-Pidal | See p. 11, n. 2. | | | |
| Morbecq | Library of the Marqués de Morbecq, Madrid | | ULC | University Library, Cambridge |

1. ALARCOS (*Conde*)
⟦ Romance del conde alarcos. |
4°. a⁴. [Sev., Crom., *c.* 1511–15.] (BM)
1*a*, col. 1: R²Etrayda esta la infãta | ...; 4*a*, col. 2: ⟦ Villancico. | ⟦ Pues q̃ mi triste penar | ...; 4*b*, col. 1: ⟦ Villancico. | ⟦ A quiẽ deuo yo llamar | ...
See Thomas, *Early*, vol. II.

2. ⟦ Romance del conde alarcos | ꝛ otro romãce de Iuan del enzina ꝛ vn villãcico a nuestra | señora nueuamente impresso. |
4°. a⁴. Composite woodcut above title. [Sev., Var., *c.* 1516–17.] (Oporto)
1*a*, col. 1: R²Etrayda esta la infanta | ...; 4*a*, in col. 2: ⟦ Romance. | Por vnos puertos arriba | ...; 4*b*, in col. 1: ⟦ Villancico. | ⟦ A quiẽ deuo yo llamar | ...

3. ⟦ Romance del conde Alarcos | ꝛ dela Infanta Solisa. Fecho por Pedro de riaño. |
⟦ Otro Romãce de Amadis: q̃ dize. Despues que el esforçado. |
4°. a⁴. Composite woodcut below title. [Sev., Crom., *c.* 1520?] (BNP)
1*a*, col. 1: ⟦ Retrayda esta la infanta ...; 4*b*, in col. 1: ⟦ Otro romã= | ce de Amadis. | ⟦ Despues que el esforçado | ...

4. ⟦ Comiēça vn roman= | ce del conde Alarcos: Hecho por Pe= | dro de riaño. |
    4°. [*]⁴. Woodcut below title. [Sar., Coci, *c.* 1520.] (BM)
1*a*, col. 1: R²Etrayda esta la infanta | ...; 4*b*, col. 1: ⟦ Villācico de guar | da me las
vacas. | ⟦ Guarda me las vacas | ...; in col. 2: ⟦ Mote. | ⟦ Pues mi vida y vīa
vida | ...
    Edited in Thomas, *Early*, vol. II.

5. AMADÍS
⟦ Romançe de amadis y oriana y | otro del rey Malsin: con otro del infante gayferos:
ꝣ otro q̄ | dize En jaen esta el buen rey. con otros dos romançes. |
    4°. [*]⁴. Woodcut below title. [Bur., Bas., 1515–17, or Mel., 1518–19.] (ULC)
1*a*, col. 1: Amadis el muy famoso | ...; 2*a*, in col. 2: Siguese vn ro= | mance del rey
Malsin. | ⁋ Ya comiēçan los franceses | ...; 3*a*, in col. 2: ⁋ Romance de gayferos. |
Media noche era passada | ...; 3*b*, col. 2: Romāce fecho ala muer | te de dõ Pedro
caruajal | y de dõ alōso su hermão. | ⁋ En jaen esta el buen rey | ...; 4*a*, in col. 1:
Otro romançe | de Nuñez. | ⁋ Por vn camino muy solo | ...: 4*b*, col. 1: Romançe
dela pre | sa de Bugia. | ⁋ En vna parte del mundo | ...
    Reproduced in this volume.

6. BURGOS (Juan de)
⟦ Otro romāce del conde claros | nueuamēte trobado por otra ma | nera. fecho por
Iuā de burgos. |
    4°. [*]². Composite woodcut below title. [Sev., Crom., *c.* 1511–15.] (BM)
1*a*, col. 1: Durmiēdo esta el cōde claros | ...
    Complete despite the wording of the title. Salvá had another copy.

7. CALAYNOS
(R³)Omāce del moro calaynos | de como req̄ria de amores | ala infanta Sebilla y ella
le | demando en arras tres cabeças | delos doze pares. |
    4°. a⁴. Composite woodcut below title. [Sev., Crom., *c.* 1511–15.] (BM)
1*a*, col. 1: ⟦ Ya caualga calaynos | ...; 4*b*, in col. 1: Coplas hechas | por juā d̄l
ēzina. | ⟦ Dos terribles pēsamiētos | ...

8. (R³)Omāce d̄l moro calaynos | de como req̄ria de amores | ala infanta sibilla: y ella
le d̄ | mando en arras tres cabeças de | los doze pares. |
    4°. [*]⁴. Composite woodcut below title. [Sev., Crom., *c.* 1520.] (BNP)
1*a*, col. 1: ⟦ Ya caualga calaynos | ...; 4*b*, in col. 1: ⟦ Villancico fe= | cho por Iuan
del enzina. | ⟦ Dos terribles pēsamiētos | ...

9. CALISTO
⟦ Romance nueuamēte hecho de Calisto y Meli | bea que trata de todos sus amores ꝣ
delas desastradas muertes suyas. ꝣ dela muerte de sus criados Sem= | pronio ꝣ parmeno:
ꝣ dela muerte de aquella desastrada muger Celestina intercessora en sus amores. |

Fº. [*]². 4 cols. Woodcut below title. [Sev., Crom., c. 1513.] (Santander)
1a, col. 1: Vn caso muy sēnalado | quiero señores contar | ...; 2b, col. 3: Villancico. |
Amor quiē đ tus plazeres | ...; col. 4: ⟨ Romāce | que fizo vn galan alaban | do a su
amiga. | ⟨ Dela luna tengo q̄xa | ...

10. CARTAS
Cartas z coplas para | requerir nueuos amo | res. |
    4º. a⁴. Bordered title-page. Composite woodcut above title, repeated on 3b. Six
    prose letters printed in long lines and each followed by verses partly in two cols.
    [Tol., Vill., c. 1515?] (Oporto)
    4b, in col. 1: Loores a vna da= | ma. | ⟨ Los altos merescimiētos | ...

11. Cartas y coplas | para req̄rir nue= | uos amores. |
    4º. [*]⁴. Single woodcuts on 1a and 3b; otherwise as no. 10. [Sev., Crom., c.
    1516–20.] (BNP)
    4b, in col. 1: Loores a vna | dama. | ⟨ Los altos merecimiētos | ...

12. COPLAS
    ¶ Aqui comiençan vnas coplas de | Iuan agraz a Iuan marmolejo. El qual sabiēdo q̄
    el dicho | juan marmolejo era aficionado al vino le da nueuas como el | vino enel año
    presente era caro...
    4º. [*]⁴. [Bur., Bas, c. 1512–15.] (BNP)
    1a, col. 1: ¶ Mala nueua dela tierra | ...; 4a, in col. 2: ¶ Coplas que hi | zo don jorge
    mārrique a vna | beuda q̄ tenia enpeñado vn | brial enla tauerna. | ¶ Han me dicho q̄
    se atreue | ...; 4b, col. 2; ¶ Coplas de vn | galan a juan poeta el qual le | imbio vn
    sayo con vn judio. | ¶ Este sayo vos embio | ...; in col. 2: ¶ Esta copla hi= | zo el
    adelantado de murcia a| vn trobador que vino a su ca | sa muy desnudo. | ¶ Poeta de
    diez en carga | ...

13. ¶ Coplas de vnos tres pastores Martin z Miguel z Antō | cō otras de Alegre fuy. z
    otras de pasesme por dios barq̄ro. |
    4º. a⁴. [Bur., Bas., 1515–17, or Mel., 1518–19.] (BNP)
    1a, col. 1: mī Iuro a sant q̄ duerma z calle | ...; 4a, col. 1: Villancico. | Triste
    fue | ...; in col. 2: Villancico. | Passa me por dios barquero | ...

14. Coplas fechas alos altos estados đlos reys nuestros | señores de como salieron a misa
    conel alteza del muy | alto principe z princesa de españa z delos caualleros | que con
    sus altezas salieron |.
    4º. [*]⁴. Title-page with bordered woodcut above title. [Bur., J. de Bur., 1496.]
    (LC)
    1b. col. 1: Alto dios omnipotente | ...
    Facsimile in *Primera floresta de incunables* (Valencia, 1957).

15. Coplas fechas por mandado de vn señor el qual tenia vn | moço adeuino y allende
    desso era perezoso mentiroso y go= | loso y sisaua le dela mercaduria que cōpraua de
    tres blan= | cas la vna: el qual tenia las tachas siguientes. |

4°. a⁴. [Bur., Bas., *c.* 1500–5.] (BNM)

1*a*, col. 1: Tengo vn moço mentiroso | ...; 3*b*, in col. 1: ⸿ Coplas hechas a vna | señora que passaua por | (col. 2) la pertenencia del ena= | morado. | Señora quando passays | ...; 4*b*, col. 1 : Vna amiga tengo hermano | ...

Facsimile in *Pliegos*, Madrid, vol. v, clxx.

16. ⸿ Coplas fechas sobre el casamiēto dela hija del Rey | despaña conel hijo del emperador duque de bergoña cō | de de flandes archiduque de autarixa.|

4°. [*]⁴. Two final woodcuts. [Bur., Bas., 1496.] (BNM)

1*a*, col. 1: Altos reyes poderosos | ...

Facsimile in *Tercera floresta de incunables* (Valencia, 1959).

17. Siguen se vnas | Coplas muy deuotas fechas | a reuerēcia del nacimiento de | nīo señor jhū cristo: ẓ cantan se | al son dela zorrilla cōel gallo. |

4°. [*]⁸ [Bur., Bas., *c.* 1499?] (Escorial, wants 2 and 7)

1*a*, col. 1: [title given above] | ⸿ El infante⸍ y el pecado | mal han barajado. | Al sereno esta el cordero | ...; 8*a*: ⸿Estas coplas son de arte mayor: y las medias coplas estan | todas en razon y por cōsonantes... (l. 4) ⸿ Con pena y cuydado⸍ continuo guerreo | ...

18. Coplas que hizo tremar a vna al | cahueta que auia engañado ciertos caualleros trayēdo los en | trespasso engañosamente. |

4°. [*]². [Sev., Crom., *c.* 1515?] (ÖNB)

1*a*, col. 1: ⸿Oyd oyd amadores | ...

19. (E³)Nlas presentes coplas se tra= | ta como vna hermosa dōzella andādo perdida por vna | montaña: encōtro con vn pastor: el qual vista su gentile | za se enamoro della...

4°, a⁴. Composite woodcut below title. [Sev., Var., *c.* 1516–17.] (Oporto)

1*a*, col. 1: ⸿ La donzella. | ⸿ Las que nascen sin ventura | ...

20. COSTANA (     )

⸿ Aqui comiēça vn conjuro de a= | mor hecho por costana con vna nao de amor: y otras co= | plas de vnos galanes maldiziendo a vna dama. |

4°. [*]⁴. Composite woodcut below title. [Bur., Bas., 1515–17, or Mel., 1518–19.] (BNP)

1*a*, col. 1: ⸿ La grandeza de mis males | ...; 3*b*, in col. 1: ⸿ Vna nao de a= | mor hecha por el comenda= | dor escriua | ⸿ De vida desamparado | ...; 4*a*, in col. 2: Del ropero a vn | portogues que lo vido vesti= | do de muchas colores. | ⸿ Dezid amigo soys flor | ...; 4*b*, in col. 1: Otra del ropero | Guardas puestas por cōsejo | ...; in col. 1: Quatro coplas | de quatro gentiles hombres | maldiziendo a vna dama. | Deforcen. | ⸿ Fe mentida humanidad | ...

21. DIDO [Lament of Dido]

⸿ Despues q̄ los griegos ₫struye | rō a troya. Eneas q̄ era troyano truxo las estatuas delos dio= | ses... (l. 7)... Finalmēte q̄ muy ₫stroça= | do y ᵽdido vino al pnerto [*sic*] de

cartago dōde reynaua helisa di= | do... (l. 12)...la reyna | como lo sintio q̄ eneas
d̄liberaua de se ptir: ēbiole esta carta lle | na de quexas....

4°. a⁴. [Sev., Crom., c. 1515?] (BM)
1 a, col. 1: ([ Eneas pues q̄ te vas | ...

22. DIODATO (Francesco)
([ Iuyzio fecho por frācisco | diodato astrologo famoso d̄la cibdad d̄ luca d̄l año | d̄
.m.d.xj. y d̄l año de .m.d.xij. Enel q̄ dize grādes co | sas q̄ hā d̄ acaecer ēnstos dos
años. y ēnspecial dela | vitoria d̄l muy alto y muy poderoso rey de hespaña |.

4°. a⁴. Diodato's *Juyzio* in prose, in long lines. [Sev., Crom., 1511?] (Norton)
4 a: ([ Iuzyio nueuamente hecho por | Pedro de frias hermitaño en roma | (col. 1)
([ El aguila q̇ere yr bolādo | ...

In the final stanza the poet calls himself Antonio de Frias.

23. DIRLOS (*Conde*)
Romançe del conde | Dirlos: y delas gran | des venturas que hu | uo. Nueuamente |
añadidas ciertas co= | sas q̄ hasta aqui no | fueron puestas. |

4°. a¹². Woodcuts flanking title. [Sar., Coci, c. 1510.] (BM)
1 a, col. 1: Estauase el conde dirlos | ...; on 12 a: A nuestra señora la virgen maria. |
su deuoto Diego Pegera. | (col. 1) ([ Oya tu merced y crea | ...; col. 2: Dize la
glosa. | Consuelo delos naçidos | ...

Edited in Thomas, *Early*, vol. 1.

24. DURANDARTE
¶ Romance de Durandarte cō | la glosa de Soria: z otros diuer= | sos Romances. |
4°. a⁴. Woodcut (from '1499' *Celestina*) below title. [Bur., Mel., c. 1520?] (Prague)
1 a, col. 1: ([ Durandarte durandarte | ...; 1 b, col. 1: Glosa d̄ soria. | ([ Dolor del
tiēpo perdido | ...; 2 a, in col. 2: ¶ Romance: | Mudado por Diego de frias | por
otro que dizen. Ya desma | yan los Franceses. | (2 b, col. 1) ([ Ya desmayan mis
seruicios | ...; 2 b, in col. 1: ¶ Romance d̄ | Garci sanchez de Badajoz. | ([ Caminan-
do por mis males | ...; 3 b, in col. 1: ¶ Otro romā= | ce de nuñez. | ([ Por vn camino
muy solo | ...; in col. 2: ¶ Romāce he= | cho por Quiros sobre los amo | res del
Marques de Zenete | con la señora Fonseca. | ([ Mi desuentura cansada | ...; 4 a, in col. 2:
¶ Otro romā= | ce hecho por Iuā del enzina. | ([ Mi libertad en sossiego | ...; 4 b, in
col. 1: ¶ Villancico | ([ Si amor pone las escalas | ...; in col. 1: ¶ Romāce he | cho
por cumillas cōtra haziē= | do al que dize: Digas me tu el | hermitaño. | ([ Digas me
tu el pensamiēto | ...

Facsimile in *Pliegos*, Praga, I, xvi.

25. ÉGLOGA
([ Egloga interlocutoria: enla qual | se introduzen tres pastores z vna zagala: llamados
Pascual: z | Benito: z Gil verto: y Pascuala. Enla qual recuēta como Pa= | scual
estaua enla sala del duque z la duquesa recontādo como ya | la seta de mahoma se
auia de apocar...

4°. a⁴. Title-page with composite woodcut above title. [Sev., Crom., *c.* 1520.] (BNP)

1*b*, col. 1: Dize Pascual. | ⟨ Dios salue aca buena gēte | …; on 4*b*: ⟨ Villancico. | (col. 1) ⟨ Demonos al alegria | …

26. ENCINA (Jerónimo del)
⟨ Testamento dela reyna doña | ysabel nueuamente trobado por | Ieronimo del enzina. |
4°. [*]². [Sev., Crom., *c.* 1511?] (BNP)
1*a*, col. 1: ⟨ Despues q̄l rey dō rodrigo | …; on 1*b*: ⟨ Iuyzio nueuamēte hecho por | Pedro de frias hermitaño en roma | (col. 1) ⟨ El aguila quiere yr bolādo | …
See note to no. 22.

27. ENCINA (Juan del)
(E⁴)Gloga representada enla noche | postrera d̄ carnal q̄ dizē de antruejo o carnes tollēdas: a dō | de se introduzen q̄tro pastores llamados Benito: y Bras: | Pedruelo: z Lloriēte…
4°. [*]⁴. [Sev., Crom., *c.* 1515?] (BNP)
1*a*, col. 1: Be. ⟨ O triste de mi cuytado | …; 3*a*, in col. 1; Egloga repēsen= | tada la mesma noche d̄ātruejo | o carnes tollēdas: a dōde se ītro | duzē los mismos pastores… | Br. Carnal fuera carnal fuera | …
Printed without the author's name.

28. E⁴Gloga trobada por Iuan del enzina. Enla qual repre | senta el Amor de como andaua a tirar en vna selua. E | de como salio vn pastor llamado Pelayo…
4°. a⁴. [Bur., Bas., 1515–17, or Mel., 1518–19.] (BNP)
1*a*, l. 7: ¶ dize el amor. | (col. 1) ¶ Ninguno tenga osadia | …; 4*b*, in col. 2: ¶ Villancico. | ¶ Ojos garços ha la niña | …

29. E³Gloga trobada por Iuan del en | zina. Enla qual representa el amor d̄ como an- | daua | a tirar en vna selua. E de como salio vn pastor lla= | mado Pelayo…
4°. [*]⁴. [Tol., Vill., *c.* 1513–20.] (Oporto)
1*a*, l. 8: Dize el amor. | (col. 1) ⟨ Ninguno tenga osadia | …; 4*b*, in col. 2: Villan- cico | ⟨ Ojos garços ha la niña | …

30. ⟨ Muchas maneras de coplas | z villancicos con el juyzio de Iuan del enzina. |
4°. [*]⁴. Composite woodcut below title. [Sev., Crom., *c.* 1511–15.] (BM)
1*a*, col. 1: ⟨ Pues amas triste amador | …; 1*b*, in col. 1: ⟨ Villancico. | ⟨ Hermitano quiero ser | …; 2*a*, in col. 1: Villancico. | Pues no te duele mi muerte | …; 2*b*, in col. 1: Vilancico. | ⟨ Pues q̄ mi triste penar | …; in col. 2: ⟨ Iuyzio fecho | por Iuā del enzina. E sacado | delo mas cierto d̄ toda la astro | logia. | ⟨ Ninguno deue dudar | …

31. ⟨ Perque de amores hecho por | Iuā del enzina: requestādo a vna gētil muger. |
4°. [*]². [Sev., Crom., *c.* 1511–15.] (BNP)
1*a*, col. 1: ⟨ Dezid vida de mi vida | …; 2*a*, in col. 1: ⟨ Iusta d̄ amo | res hecha por

Iuā del ēzina a | vna dōzella q̄ mucho le pena | ua la q̄l đ su pena q̇so doler se | Pues por vos crece mi pena | . . .

32. FERDINAND V, *King of Spain*
⟨ Elegia: fecha ala muerte đl catho | lico rey don Fernando de gloriosa memoria. Enla qual se haze men= | cion delo mas substancial de su testamento. |
    4°. [*]². [Sev., Var., 1516?] (Oporto)
    1 *a*, col. 1: Y²A estaua p̄tida đ mi pēsamiēto: | . . .

33. GARCISÁNCHEZ DE BADAJOZ
⟨ Infierno de amadores que fizo | Garcisanches de badajoz. |
    4°. [*]⁴. [Sev., Crom., *c.* 1511–15.] (BNP)
    1 *a*, col. 1: ⟨ Como en veros me perdi | . . .

34. ⟨ Las maldiciōes dichas clara | escura đl mismo garcisanchez de badajoz: comiēça eñsta māera |.
    4°. [*]². [Sev., Crom., *c.* 1511–15.] (ÖNB)
    1 *a*, col. 1: ⟨ El dia infelix noturno | . . .; 1 *b*, in col. 1: ⟨ Sueño fecho | porel mismo garcisanchez cu | yo comiēço es este. | ⟨ La mucha tristeza mia | . . .; on 2 *a*: ⟨ Glosa del romance por el mes | era de Mayo. Que hizo garcisanchez de badajoz estādo pre | so en vna torre. La q̄l embio a su amiga. dize el romāce assi. | (col. 1) ⟨ Porel mes era de mayo | . . .; in col. 2: ⟨ Comiença la | glosa del cada dos pies del ro | mance en vna copla. | (2 *b*, col. 1) ⟨ Si de amor libre estuuiera | . . .

35. ⟨ Las maldiciones dichas clara escura | del mismo garcisanches de badajoz comiençan enesta ma= | nera. |
    4°. a². [Tol., Vill., *c.* 1515?] (BNP. Oporto)
    1 *a*, col. 1: ⟨ El dia infelix no turno | . . .; 1 *b*, in col. 1: ⟨ Sueño fecho | por el mismo garcisāchez cu | yo comienço es este. | ⟨ La mucha tristeza mia | . . .; on 2 *a*: Glosa del romance por el mes era de= | Mayo. Que hizo Garcisanchez de badajoz estando preso ē | en [*sic*] vna torre. La qual embio a su amiga: dize el romāce assi | (col. 1) ⟨ Por el mes era de mayo | . . .; 2 *b*, col. 1: [*gloss*] ⟨ Si đ amor libre estuuiera | . . .

36. GAYFEROS
⟨ Romance de don gayferos que trata de como saco a su espo- | sa que estaua en tierra de moros. |
    F°. [*]². 3 cols. [Sev., Crom., *c.* 1513?] (Santander)
    1 *a*, col. 1: ⟨ Assentado esta Gayferos | . . .

37. ⟨ Romāce de don gayferos q̄ tra | ta de como saco a su esposa que estaua en tierra de moros. |
    4°. a⁴. [Sev., Crom., *c.* 1511–15.] (BM)
    1 *a*, col. 1: ⟨ Assentado esta gayferos | . . .
        See Thomas, *Early*, vol. III.

38. ⟦ Romāce de don Gayferos | que trata de como saco a su esposa que estaua en tierra de moros. |
  4°. a⁴. Woodcut below title. [Sev., Crom., *c.* 1511-15.] (BM. Morbecq)
  1 a, col. 1: ⟦ Assentado esta gayferos | ...
    Edited in Thomas, *Early*, vol. III. Facsimile in *Pliegos*, Morbecq, pp. 125-32.

39 GRACIOSO
  (G⁴)racioso razonamiēto en que se | introduzē dos rufianes el vno pregūtādo el otro respondiēdo en germania de sus vidas ꝛ arte đ | biuir...
  4°. a⁴. Composite woodcut above title. In single column, with marginal indications of the intervention of each character, with a woodcut figure, not always appropriate, below or in the opposite margin. [Sev., Var., *c.* 1518-19.] (Oporto)
  1 a, l. 10: ⟦ A boca de sorna por yr encubierto | ...

40. GUARINOS (*Conde*)
  (R⁴)Omance del conde guari= | nos almirante dela mar⸋ nueuamente trobado | como lo catiuarō moros Y vnas coplas de ma | dalenica. |
  4°. [*]². [Sev., Crom., *c.* 1511-15.] (BNP)
  1 a, col. 1: ⟦ Mal ouistes los frāceses | ...; 2 a, in col. 2: Coplas de ma= | dalenica. | ⟦ Abras me madalenica | ...

41. GUILLÉN DE ÁVILA (Diego)
  ⟦ Egloga interlocutoria: graciosa y por gē | til estilo nueuamente trobada por diego de | auila: dirigida al muy illustrissimo gran ca= | pitan. | ...
  4°. a⁸b⁸c². Alc. [S. Polono, *c.* 1502-4.] (No copy located)
  [2 a: Egloga, presumably beginning, as in a lost edition in F. Colón's *Regestrum*, no. 3852, 'No puede ser mayor maldicion'. On 17 b: Unas coplas pastoriles para cantar, de como dos pastores andando con su ganado rogava el un pastor al otro le mostrase rezar el pater noster...fecha por Rodrigo de Reynosa.]
    See p. 8, n. 1.

42. JEREZ DE LA FRONTERA
  ⟦ Coplas hechas sobre vn caso | acontescido en Xerez dela frontera de vn hombre q̄ mato ve= | ynte y dos personas a traycion. |
  4°. [*]². [Sev., Crom., *c.* 1515?] (BNP)
  1 a, col. 1: ⟦ Gentes de todas naciones | ...; 2 b, in col. 1: ⟦ Cancion q̄ se | cāta al tono de los comēdado | res por mi mal os vi. | (col. 2) Casa mōte alegre por mal te vierō | los tristes cuytados q̄ ē ti murierō. | ...

43. JESUS CHRIST
  ⟦ Coplas hechas ala natiuidad | de nuestro señor Iesu xp̄o: nueua mente hechas. |
  4°. [*]². [Sev., Crom., *c.* 1515?] (BNP)
  1 a, col. 1: ⟦ Venida es venida | al mundo la vida. | ...

44. JUYZIO
Iuyzio hallado y trobado para emienda | de nuestras vidas delas cosas que en nuestros dias hā de acon | tecer...
    4°. a⁶. [Sal., Porr., *c.* 1510?] (ULC)
1*a*, col. 1: ⟪ Dela llena delos rios | ...
        Reproduced in this volume.

45. LÓPEZ DE YANGUAS (Hernán)
Triumphos de locura | nueuamēte compue= | stos por Hernan | lopez de yan | guas .:. |
    4°. a¹². Woodcut on title-page below title. [Bur., Mel., *c.* 1520.] (BM, wants 11; Morbecq, wants 3–8)
2*a*, col. 1: P²Ensando como es razon | ...
        Facsimile in *Pliegos*, Morbecq, pp. 135–55. For an edition in eight leaves printed by J. Joffre in Valencia in 1521 see Rodríguez-Moñino's introduction, p. 45. Its more spacious printing suggests that the present edition may be earlier; typographically it is of the years 1519–23.

46. MADALENICA
⟪ Coplas de Madalenica. | ⟪ Otras de tābuē ganadico aña | didas por Iaques normante. | ⟪ Otros fieros que hizo vn rufiā | en çamora con vna puta. |
    4°. A⁴. [Sev., Crom., *c.* 1511–15.] (BM. BNP)
1*a*, col. 1: ⟪ Tambuen ganadico | y mas en tal valle | ...; 2*a*: ⟪ Coplas hechas por Aluaro de | solana. En que cuenta como en | çamora vido hazer a vn rufian cō | vna puta los fieros siguientes. | (col. 1) El. | ⟪ Yo te voto a dios ximena | ...; 3*b*, in col. 1: ⟪ Villancico. | ⟪ Pues el fin de mi esperāça | ...; in col. 2: Comiençan las | coplas de Madalenica. | (4*a*, col. 1) ⟪ Abras me madalenica | ...; 4*b*, in col. 1: ⟪ Villancico. | ⟪ No te tardes q̄ me muero | carcelero | ...

47. ⟪ Coplas de Madalenica. | Otras de tam buen ganadico aña | didas por. Iaques normante. | Otros fieros que hizo vn rufian | en çamora con vna puta. |
    4°. A⁴. [Sev., Var., *c.* 1515–19.] (Oporto, two copies)
(As no. 46, except: 2*a*: ...en ça | mora...rufiā cō vna | puta. los...; 3*b*, in col. 1: ⟪ villancico. | ...; 3*b*, in col. 2: ...las. | coplas...; 4*b*, in col. 1: ⟪ villancico. | ...

48. MANRIQUE (Jorge)
⟪ Coplas q̄ hizo don Iorge mā= | rrique ala muerte del maestre de santiago don rodrigo mārri= | que su padre. |
    4°. [*]⁴. Woodcut at head of col. 1 of text. [Sev., Crom., *c.* 1512?] (BNP)
1*a*, col. 1: ⟪ Recuerde el alma dormida | ...

49. [El pater noster de las mugeres trobado en castellano por don Jorge Manrique con otras coplas.]
    4°. a⁴. [Tol., Vill., *c.* 1515–20.] (Rodríguez-Moñino, wants 1 and 4)
2*a*, in col. 1: [*Pater noster* ends] seamos dellas pagados | Amen. | Vn combite que |

hizo don Iorge manrique a su | madrastra. | ⟨ Señora muy acabada | ...; 3 *a*, in col. 1:
Aqui comiença el | Nique. | ⟨ Nunca vi descanso cierto | ...; [4, with poems by
A. de Montoro, not known].

See p. 93 of Rodrĩguez-Moñino's *Noticias bibliográficas* accompanying the
Spanish Academy's fascimile of the 1511 *Cancionero general*. The title given
above is taken by Professor Rodríguez-Moñino from Fernando Colón's
description (*Regestrum* 4115) of a copy of this edition, or of a close reprint,
bought at Medina del Campo in 1524.

50. MANTUA (*Marqués de*)
⟨ Aqui comiençan dos romã | ces del marques de mantua. El primero es de como an |
dãdo pdido por vn bosque fallo a su sobrino Baldoui | nos cõ feridas de muerte. Y el
segũdo la embaxada q̃ el | marques embio al empador demãdando justicia. E o= | tro
agora añadido q̃ es la sentẽcia q̃ dierõ a Carloto: fe | cha por Ieronymo tremiño de
Calatayud. |
4°. a [and A]¹². Woodcut below title. [Vall.? Broc., *c.* 1515–19.] (BNP)
1 *a*, col. 1: D²E mãtua salio el marq̃s | ...; 7 *a*, in col. 1: Romance dela | embaxada
que embio da= | nes vger al empador. | D²E mantua salen apriessa | ...; 10 *b*, in
col. 2: Sentencia da= | da contra Carloto. | ⟨ Enel nombre de jesus | ...

51. MARTÍN (*Fray* Andrés)
⟨ Coplas dela missa đ nuestra se | ñora: desde el principio đla cõfession fasta el ite
missa est: fechas | por vn reuerẽdo frayle đla orden đ sant frãcisco. |
4°. a⁴. [Sev., Crom., *c.* 1511–15.] (ÖNB)
1 *a*, col. 1: ⟨ Con asaz temor prosigo | ...; 4 *b*, in col. 2, ends: ...y fago fin | vn
pobrezillo doctor | item mas frayle menor | dicho fray andres martin. |

52. MARY, *the Blessed Virgin*
Aue maria trobada por vn de | uoto frayle: indigno seruidor | suyo...
4°. [*]⁴. Woodcut at head of first column, followed by title. [Tol., Vill., *c.* 1513–
20.] (Oporto)
1 *a*, in col. 1: ⟨ Aue reyna gloriosa | ...; 2 *b*: ⟨ Prosa o modo de suplicaciõ q̃ haze vn
deuoto... (l. 8, col. 1) ⟨ Reyna sin comparacion | ...

53. ⟨ Coplas sobre el a | ue maria trobadas | por vn religioso de | sant Iheronimo. |
4°. [*]⁴. Bordered title-page, with woodcut above title. [Sev., Crom., *c.* 1511–15.]
(ÖNB)
1 *b*, col. 1: Aue | ⟨ Aue rosa speciosa | ...

54. ⟨ La salue regina | muy deuota troba | da por vn religioso | de sã Iheronimo. |
4°. [*]⁴. Woodcut above title. [Sev., Crom., *c.* 1511–15.] (ÖNB)

1 *a*, col. 1: Introducion. | ⟦ Aquesta salue regina | . . .; 1 *b*, in col. 2: La salue regina | Salue. | ⟦ Salue nr̄a saluaciō | . . .; 4 *b*, in col. 2: El versito. ora | pro nobis .z̄c̄. con su responso | trobado en vna copla. | ⟦ Rogad por nos de cōtino | . . .

55. MELISENDA

A²Qui comiẽça el romance dela Melisen | da hija del emperador y trata delas tray | ciones y encantamẽtos que hizo por amores | del conde Ayuelos con vna metafora de Qui | ros hecha a Iuan fernandez de eredia. |

 4º. a⁴. Composite woodcut below title. [Bur., Bas., 1515–17, or Mel., 1518–19.] (BNP)

1 *a*, col. 1: ¶ Todas las gentes dormiā | . . .; 2 *a*, in col. 2: Romāce de garci san | ches de badajos. | ¶ Caminādo por mis males | . . .; 2 *b*, in col. 2: Metafora en metros | q̄ fizo Quiros al señor Iuan | fernandez deredia siendo ser | uidor đla señora Geronima | beneyta: estādo ella en vn lu | gar que se llama Alcaçar. | ¶ Entre valencia y alcaçar | . . .; 4 *b*, in col. 1: Copla de Anton de | mōtoro a vn portugues q̄ vi | do vestido đ muchas colores | ¶ Dezid hermāo soys flor | . . .; in col. 1: Romāce đ durādarte | ¶ Durandarte durandarte | . . .; in col. 2: Otro romance. | ¶ Mudado se el pēsa-miēto | . . .

56. MENDOZA (*Fray* Íñigo de)

⟦ Los gozos đ nuestra señora la | virgen Maria cōpuestos por fray iñigo de mēdoça. |

 4º. [*]⁴. Woodcuts below title and on 3 *b*. [Sev., Crom., *c.* 1515?] (BNP)

1 *a*, col. 1: ⟦ Emperatriz delos dos | . . .; 3 *b*, col. 1: ⟦ Preguntas a | nuestra señora la virgen ma= | ria. | [woodcut] | Madre reyna poderosa | . . .; 4 *b*, col. 2: ⟦ Villancico. | ⟦ Quien touiere por señora | . . .

 Facsimile in *Tercera floresta de incunables* (Valencia, 1959).

57. MONTESINO (*Fray* Ambrosio)

⟦ Coplas hechas por fray ambrosio mō= | tesino dela coluna del señor. por ruego dela muy magnifica se= | ñora la condessa de curuña. |

 4º. a⁶. Woodcut above title. [Tol., Hag. succ., *c.* 1510?] (BNP)

1 *a*, col. 1: ⟦ Por grande gloria rescibo | . . .; on 5 *b*: Fray ambrosio mōtesino hizo estas co= | plas de lamentaciō sobre estar el rey del cielo solo atado z aço | tado en la coluna. Cāta se al son q̄ dizē. Q [*sic*] castillo đ mōtāches | (col. 1) ⟦ O coluna de pilato | . . .

58. ⟦ Coplas hechas sobre la | passiō de nuestro señor Ie | su christo. |

 4º. [*]². Woodcuts above title and at end. [Sev., Crom., *c.* 1511–15.] (BNP)

1 *a*, col. 1: ⟦ El rey dela gloria | . . .

 Without any note of authorship.

59. MONTESINOS

⟦ Romance de vn desafio q̄ se hi= | zo en paris de dos cauallŕos prin= | cipales đla tabla redōda: los qua= | les son montesinos z oliueros: fue | el siguiēte desafio por amores de | vna dama q̄ se llamaua Aliarda. |

 4º. [*]⁴. [Sev., Crom., *c.* 1511–15.] (BNP)

1 *a*, col. 1: E²Nnlas [*sic*] salas de paris | ...; 4*a*, col. 1: Coplas hechas | por juan del enzina. | ⟪ Razō que fuerça no q̃ere | ...; 4*b*: ⟪ Villācico hecho por el marques | de sātillana a vnas tres hijas suyas. | (col. 1) ⟪ Por vna gentil floresta | ...

60. MORAYMA
(R⁵)Omāce dela Mora mo | rayma: glosado. ⟪ Otro romance que dize Por | mayo era por mayo: glosado. Otro romance de | Garcisanchez de badajoz que dize. Caminādo por | mis males. Otro romance đ dō Iuan manuel que | dize Gritando va el cauallero. ⟪ Otro romance del comēdador | Auila que dize. Descubra se el pensamiento. |
    4°. a⁴. [Sev., Crom., *c.* 1520?] (Prague)
1 *a*, col. 1: ⟪ Yo mera mora morayma | ...; in col. 1: Glosa de pinar | a este romance | (col. 2) ⟪ Quando mas embeuecida | ...; 2*a*, in col. 1: Otro romance. | Que por mayo era por mayo | ...; in col. 2: Glosa de nico= | las nuñez. | ⟪ En mi desdicha se cobra | ...; 2*b*, in col. 2: ⟪ Romāce de | Garcisanches de badajoz. | ⟪ Caminando por mis males | ...; 3*b*, in col. 2: Romāce de | don Iuan manuel | ⟪ Gritādo va el cauallero | ...; 4*a*, in col. 2: ⟪ Otro romā= | ce del comendador Auila | (4*b*, col. 1) ⟪ Descubrase el pensamiento | ...; in col. 2: Desecha. | ⟪ Consolaos males es- quiuos | ...
    Facsimile in *Pliegos*, Praga, I, xxxv.

61. ORAN
Carta dela grā victoria | y presa de Oran. Enla qual se contiene la for | ma y manera de como es estada ganada. Con vnas que dizen la | misma victoria. Con dos villāçetes por muy gentil estilo. |
    4°. [*]². Woodcut below title. [Bar., Amor., 1509.] (March. Norton)
1 *b*, l. 17 [after the prose letter]: Vilançico. | (col. 1) Por que dubdas Reduam | ...; in col. 2: Coplas đ como gana | ron a Oran. | (2*a*, col. 1) ⟪ O grā nueua que es venida | ...; 2*b*, in col. 2: Vilançico | ¶ O senyor omnipotente | ...

62. ORTIZ (Andrés)
Romance nueuamēte he | cho por andres ortiz en q̃ se | tratan los amores de Flo | riseo: y dela reyna de bo= | hemia. |
    4°. a⁴. Bordered title-page, with woodcut above title. [Sev., Crom. *c.*1520.](BNP)
1 *b*, col. 1: ⟪ Quien vuiesse tal ventura | ...

63. PAREDES (*Conde de*)
⟪ Coplas đl cōde de parades [*sic*] a | juā poeta tornadizo q̃ndo lo catiuarō sobre mar y lo lleuarō | a allēde: y como se torno moro. Y otras al mismo juā poeta en | vna p̃donāça en Valēcia. Y otras coplas de Mōtoro. |
    4°. a⁴. Woodcut below title. [Sev., Crom., *c.* 1512.] (BNP)
1 *a*, col. 1: ⟪ Si no lo quereys negar | ...; 3*a*, in col. 2: Coplas đl con= | de de paredes a Iuā poeta en | vna p̃donāça en Valēcia. | ⟪ Iuā poeta en vos venir | ...; 4*a*, in col. 2: ⟪ Otra đl rope= | ro a Iuā muñiz porq̃ le vido | tener nouenas en santa maria |

delas dueñas. | ⟨ No lo digo por blasfemia | . . . ; 4*b*, col. 1: ⟨ Otra de otro | trobador a vna dama fea. | ⟨ Visarma del tiēpo viejo | . . . ; in col. 1: ⟨ Sola de antō | de mōtoro al corregidor đ cor | doua porq̄ no hallo ēla carne | ceria sino tocino y ouo de con | prar del. | ⟨ Vno delos verdaderos | . . . ; in col. 1: ⟨ Otra suya a | vn prior. | ⟨ Serenissimo señor | . . . ; in col. 2: Otra suya al con | destable por vn saualo. | ⟨ Cōdestable muy amado | . . . ; in col. 2: ⟨ Otra đl rope= | ro a dos mugeres la vna pu= | ta: y la otra beoda. | ⟨ Aueros de bastecer | . . .

64. PEDRAZA (Cristóbal de)
⟨ Coplas hechas por Christoual | de Pedraza criado đl illustre y muy magnifico señor Duque de | Arcos. para cantar la gloriosissima noche de nauidad alos may | tines. Con vna aue Maria al cabo nueuamente trobada sobre | cada palabra vna copla. |
4°. a⁴. Composite woodcut above title. [Sev., Var., *c.* 1517–18.] (Oporto)
1*a*, col. 1: ⟨ Al tono de Abras | me tu el hermitaño. | ⟨ Alegrias alegrias | . . . [and six more Christmas poems]; 3*b*, col. 2: ⟨ El aue Maria | en coplas sobre cada pala | bra vna copla. | Aue. | ⟨ Aue. aue que bolaste | . . . ; 4*b*, in col. 1: ⟨ Villancico a nue- | stra señora. | ⟨ No ay palabras q̄ declaren | . . .
Facsimile by A. Pérez Gómez, [Cieza] Christmas 1962.

65. QUIRÓS ( )
(M⁵)Etafora en metros: que | fizo Quiros al señor Iu | an fernandez deredia si= | endo seruidor dela seño= | ra geronima Benyta e= | stando ella en vn lugar que se llama al | caçar. |
4°. a⁴. [Tol., Vill., *c.* 1515?] (Oporto)
1*a*, col. 1: ⟨ Entre valencia y alcaçar | . . . ; 3*b*, in col. 1: ⟨ Perque de Qui= | ros despidiendose de vnos a= | migos suyos | ⟨ Señores q̄ me mandays | . . . ; 4*a*, in col. 2: ⟨ Canciō del comē | dador estuñiga đ macho y hē | bra. | ⟨ Tristura comigo va | . . .

66. REPREHENSION
R²Eprehension de vicios y estados en gene | ral conpuesto por vn religioso de obser | uancia a honor de Iesu christo: y consolacion | del q̄ se quisiere exercitar en tenerle por espejo. |
4°. a⁴. [Sar., Coci, *c.* 1520?] (BM)
1*a*, col. 1: ⟨ Nadie siente tal dolor | . . . ; 3*b*, in col. 1: ⟨ Diuerso compuesto por | Iñigo Beltran de valde= | lomar. | ⟨ Peca de gran necedad | quien dize mal de mugeres | . . . ; 4*b*, col. 1: ⟨ Disparates. | ⟨ En vnos montes espessos | . . .

67. REYNOSA (Rodrigo de)
A³Qui comiēçan vnas coplas delas coma= | dres. Fechas a ciertas comadres no tocando enlas | buenas: saluo digo delas malas y de sus lenguas ⁊ ha | blas malas: y de sus afeytes y de sus azeytes ⁊ blanduras ⁊ de | sus trajes ⁊ otros sus tratos. Fechas por Rodrigo đ reynosa. |
4°. A¹². [Bur., Bas., 1517–17, or Mel., 1518–19.] (BNP)
1*a*, col. 1: ⁋ Fuestes oy comadre amissa | . . .

68. ⟪ Comiençan vnas coplas đ vn | pastor: ꝫ vna hija de vn labrador. Cantan se al tono de vna | amiga tengo hermano. Fechas por rodrigo de reynosa. |

    4°. a². Composite woodcut at head of first column. [Sev., Crom., *c.* 1520.] (BNP) 1*a*, col. 1: Dize el pastor. | [woodcut] | ⟪ Aborrir quiero antonilla | ...; 1*b*, col. 2: ⟪ Villancico. | ⟪ Los tus ojos regordidos | ...; 2*a*, col. 1: ⟪ Villancico pa | ra cantar. Fecho por rodrigo | de reynosa a su amiga. | ⟪ Iamas puede ser vencido | ...; 2*b*, col. 1: ⟪ Comiēçan v | nas coplas fechas por Rodri | go de reynosa a su amiga quā | do estuuo doliente de ciciones. | ⟪ Yo tengo gran pensamiēto | ...

69. (C⁴)Omiēçan vnas coplas pa= | storiles para cantar de como dos pastores andan= | do cō su ganado rogaua el vn pastor al otro le mo= | strasse rezar el pater noster: que ellos en su lengua= | je pastoril llaman patarniega. Fechas por Rodrigo de rey= | nosa. |

    4°. [*]². [Sev., Crom., *c.* 1520.] (BNP) 1*a*, col. 1: ⟪ Daca mingo rauia en ti | ...; 2*a*: ⟪ Comiençan vnas coplas đ co | mo el auctor que las fizo quiere loar a su amiga de todas las | gracias que tiene. El qual auctor es el dicho Rodrigo de rey | nosa. | (col. 1) ⟪ Con vuestro plazer | ...

70. (A³)Qui comiençan vnas coplas q̄ | se dizē si te vas bañar juanica y han se de cantar al tho | no [de] los vuestros cabellos niña .ꝫ.c̄. Fechas por ro | drigo de Reynosa.∴ |

    4°. [*]⁴. [Sev., Var., *c.* 1515–19.] (Oporto) 1*a*, col. 1: ⟪ Si te vas vañar juanica | ...; 1*b*, in col. 1: Comiençan otr= | as suyas ꝑa las q̄ son enamora | (col. 2) das: hā se [*sic*] cātar al tono de fas= | ta la venida q̄ vēga me atēded | Fechas por rodrigo đ reinosa | Donzella do amor esta | ...; 2*a*, in col. 2: ⟪ Otras suyas a | vna moça por q̄ enel año dela | hābre de mill ꝫ quiniētos ꝫ se | ys ala q̄l reqria đ amores porq̄ | se enamoro de sus ojos y el los | loaua: y ella dezia q̄ mas q̄ria | Pan fechas por Rodrigo de | Reynosa auctor.∴ | Gentiles ojos aueys niña | ...; 3*a*, in col. 2: Coplas de amo= | res ꝑa cātar fechas a ruego ꝫ | yntercessiō de vn cātor del ilus | tre ꝫ manifico señor dō Alua= | ro de estuñiga prior de san Iu | an llamado quītana. Fechas | por rodrigo de reynosa. | ⟪ Gran deporte es el amor | ...; 3*b*, in col. 2: Aqui comiençan | vnas coplas. Fechas por vn | (4*a*, col. 1) bachiller para su amiga en q̄ | el le pedia por merced q̄ pues | se dezia que era su amiga que | fuesse assi y van al tono de de= | manda me carillo q̄ a ti dar te | me hā ꝫ.c̄. Fechas por Ro= | drigo de reynosa.∴ | ⟪ Por que sea satisfecho | ...; in col. 2: ⟪ villancico por | desecha.∴ | ⟪ Alça la boz el pregonero | ...; in col. 2: Cancion.∴ | No puede sanar ventura | ...; 4*b*, in col. 1: Romançe que hi | zo nuñez que dize dezi me vos | penssamiento: | ...; in col. 2: ⟪ villācico. | El dia de alegria | ...

71. ⟪ Aqui comiēça vn pater noster tro= | babo [*sic*] y dirigido alas damas. Y las coplas dela chinagala. Y | vn villancico que dize. Los cabellos de mi amiga de oro son. | Con otras de vn ventero ꝫ vn escudero. Y vn villancico que | dize. No tenga [*sic*] vida segura en no ver su hermosura. Troba= | do por Rodrigo de reynosa. |

    4°. a⁴. Woodcut below title. [Bur., Mel., *c.* 1520.] (BNM)

1 *a*, col. 1: [[ O señor pues te tenemos | ...; 2 *b*: ¶ Ala chinagala la gala chinela. | (col. 1) [[ De mas cortesanas | ...; 3 *a*, in col. 1: ¶ Coplas avn vi= | llancico viejo que dize. | (col. 2) [[ Los cabellos de mi amiga | ...; in col. 2: ¶ Coplas de vn | ventero y vn escudero he= | chas por Rodrigo de rey | nosa. | [[ Acojeme aca esta noche | ...; 4 *b*, col. 2: ¶ Villancico he= | cho por Rodrigo đ reynosa. | [[ No tengo vida segura |...
  Facsimiles by J. Sancho Rayón [Madrid, 187–], and in *Pliegos*, Madrid, ii, xlvii.

72. Comienza vn razona | miento por coplas en que se cō= | trahaze la jermania z fieros de | los rufianes z las mugeres del | partido: z de vn rufian llama= | do cortauiento: y ella catalina | torres altas. Fechas por rodri= | go đ reynosa. |
  4°. [*]². Bordered title-page. [Tol., Hag. succ., *c.* 1505–10?] (BNP)
  1 *b*, col. 1: Dize el rufian | [[ Catalina de mi querida | ...

73. [[ Comiença vn tratado hecho por co= | plas sobre q̄ vna señora embio a pedir por merced al auctor | que las hizo que pues estaua de parto le embiase algun re= | medio. el qual le responde por coplas. Han se de cantar al to | no de rezeinos beatus vir zc. El qual autor es llamado ro= | drigo de reynosa. |
  4°. [*]². Composite woodcut above title. [Tol., Vill., *c.* 1515?] (BNP)
  1 *a*, col. 1: Dize la muger al marido. | [[ Llamame ala comadre | ...

74. ROCH (*St*)
  C²Oplas hechas por vn religioso de | la orden de sant. Augustin del bien | auenturado sant Roch: conformes a su | hystoria: para excitar a las gentes a mas | deuocion: en especial para que le llamen | en tiempo dela pestilencia: que es santo | muy apropiado para libra de tal necessi= | dad. y comiēçan assi hablādo a sāt Roch. |
  4°. [*]⁴. Title-page with woodcut below title, others on 3 *a*, 4 *a*. [Tol., Vill., *c.* 1513–20.] (Oporto)
  1 *b*., col. 1: [[ Tanta fue vuestra bondad | ...; 3 *a*: Siguese otra obra contemplatiua: sobre | lo que dize sant juan que la señora estaua | al pie dela cruz mirando su hijo bendito. | y dize. | [woodcut] | (col. 1) [[ A quien miraran mis ojos | ...; 4 *a*: Siguese la hystoria trobada del niño je= | su cristo perdido eñl templo de edad de | doze años: sacada del euangelio de sant | lucas. | [woodcut] | (col. 1) Dize nuestra señora. | [[ Pues el niño no paresce | ...

75. ROMANCE
  [...] Ro= | [mance de los doze pares de Fran] | çia por muy | [gentil estilo...]
  4°. [*]⁴. Composite woodcut below title. [Bar., Ros., *c.* 1513–20.] (G. Menéndez-Pidal)
  1 *a*, col. 1: [En missa esta] el emperador | ...; 3 *a*, in col. 1: [*Romance del palmero*; beginning lost]; 3 *b*, col. 1: Villançico. | ¶ Cuydado no me congoxes | ...; in col. 1: [*Romance* on the death of Philip I; beginning lost]; 4 *a*, in col. 2: [...] romançe de Iu= | [an del E]nzina. | [Por vnos] puertos arriba| ...; 4 *b*, in col. 1: Otro Ro-

man[çe.] | (( Caminando sin [plazer] | ...; in col. 2: [a *villancico*, beginning and end lost].

> Defective copy, from a binding. Text edited in F. J. Sánchez-Cantón, 'Un pliego de romances desconocido, de los primeros años del siglo XVI' in *Revista de filología española*, VII (1920), 37–46.

76. ¶ Romance nueuo por muy gentil | estilo: con vna glosa nueua al romance q̄ dize En castillla [*sic*] | esta vn castillo que se llama rocha frida. Y el romāce de a [*sic*] | reyna Elena. Y vnas coplas y villancicos. |

> 4°. a⁴. Woodcut below title. [Bur., Mel., *c.* 1520?] (Prague)
> 1*a*, col. 1: (( Por vn bosq̄ tenebroso | ...; 2*a*, in col. 1: Otra glosa suya. | (( Porq̄ en tal caso y tenor | ...; 2*b*, in col. 2; Villancico suyo. | (( Porq̄ me beso perico | ...; 3*a*, in col. 1: ¶ Romāce dela | Reyna Elena. | Reyna elena reyna elena | ...; 4*a*, in col. 1: ¶ Coplas q̄ hizo | vn gentil hōbre a su amiga. | (col. 1) (( Bendito sea aquel dia | ...; 4*b*, in col. 2: ¶ Mote. | (( Pues mi vida τ vr̄a vida | ...
> Facsimile in *Pliegos*, Praga, II, lxxi.

77. ROMANCES

> ¶ Siguēse dos romances por muy | gentil estilo. El primero delos doze | pares de francia. El segundo del cō | de Guarinos almirante dela mar. τ | trata como lo cautiuaron moros. |
>
> 4°. [*]⁴. Woodcut below title and on 3*b*. [Bur., Bas., 1515–17, or Mel., 1518–19.] (BM)
>
> 1*a*, col. 1: En missa esta el emperador | ...; 3*a*, in col. 2: Romance del Conde | guarinos almirāte dla mar τ | trata como lo catiuarō moros | (3*b*) [woodcut] | (col. 1) ¶ Mala vistes los franceses | ...
> Edited in Thomas, *Thirteen*.

78. A²Qui comiēçan onze maneras de romā= | ces. Con sus villancetes y aqueste prime | ro romance fue fecho al Conde de oliua. |

> 4°. [*]⁴. Woodcut below title. [Bur., Bas., 1515–17, or Mel., 1518–19.] (BM)
> 1*a*, col. 1: ¶ Yo me parti de valencia | ...; 1*b*, in col. 1: Otro romance. | ¶ Estando en contemplaciō | ...; in col. 2: Desecha. | ¶ Coraçō procura vida | ...; in col. 2: Este romance hizo | don diego de acuña. | ¶ Alterado el pensamiento | ...; 2*a*, in col. 1: Desecha. | ¶ Lloren mis ojos | ...; in col. 1: Este romance añadio | quiros desde dōde dize ques | de ti señora mia. | ¶ Triste estaua el cauallero | ...; in col. 2: Villancico. | ¶ Cuydado no me cōgoxes | ...; 2*b*, in col. 1: Otro romançe viejo | hasta dōde dize mi vida quie | ro hazer: y de ay adelante ha | ze Quiros. | ¶ Amara yo vna señora | ...; 2*b*, in col. 2: Villancico. | ¶ Que vida terna sin vos | ...; in col. 2: Este romāce hizo qui | ros al Marques de arzene= | ta por los amores dela seño= | ra fonseca. | ¶ Mi desuentura cansada | ...; 3*b*, col. 1: Otro romance de dō | Tristan de leonis. | ¶ Ferido esta don tristan | ...; in col. 2: Otro romance de vn | cauallero đ como le traē nue | uas q̄ su amiga era muerta. | ¶ Enlos tiempos que me vi | ...;

4*a*, in col. 1: Romance de vn caua | llero como pregunta a su pē | samiento y dela respuesta. | ¶ Dezime vos pensamiēto | ...; in col. 2: Desecha. | ¶ El dia del alegria | ...; in col. 2: Mote. | ¶ Quiē quisiere q̄ la muerte | ...; 4*b*: Siguese vn romance de vna gen | til dama y vn rustico pastor.∴ | (col. 1) ¶ Estase la gentil dama | ...; in col. 2: Otro romance. | ¶ Rosa fresca rosa fresca | ...
  Edited in Thomas, *Thirteen.*

79. ⟦ Aqui comiençan .iij. Roman= | ces Glosados. y este primero dize. Catiuaron me | los Moros. y otro⸲ ala Bella mal marida= | da. y otro. Caminando por mis males. | Con vn Villancico. |
  4°. a⁴. Composite woodcut below title, another on 3*b*. [Sev., Crom., *c.* 1520. (BNP)
  1*a*, col. 1: ⟦ En mi juuentud passada | ...; 2*a*, in col. 2: ⟦ Villancico. | ⟦ Pues el consejo del padre | ...; 2*b*, in col. 1: ⟦ Romance de | la bella mal maridada. | ⟦ La bella mal maridada | ...; in col. 2: Glosa de q̄sada. | ⟦ Quando amor en mi ponia | ...; 3*b*, in col. 1: ⟦ Glosa sobre el | Romance que dize. Cami= | nando por mis males. | (col. 2) [woodcut] | ⟦ Viendo que mi pensamiento | ...; 4*b*, in col. 2: ⟦ Villancico. | ⟦ Dama cogida en tu hato | ...

80. SAN PEDRO (Diego de)
  ⟦ Las siete angustias de nr̄a seño | ra la virgen Maria. Fechas por diego de sant pedro. |
  4°. a⁴. Woodcut at head of first column. [Sev., Crom., *c.* 1511–15.] (BNP)
  1*a*, col. 1: ⟦ Virgen digna de alabāça | ...

81. SIERRA BERMEJA
  ⟦ Deshecha sobre lo acaescido ē= | la sierra bermeja y đlos lugares perdidos. Tiene la sonada đ | los comēdadores. |
  4°. [*]⁴. Woodcut below title. [Sev., Crom., *c.* 1511–15.] (BM)
  1*a*, col. 1: ⟦ Ay sierra bermeja | por mi mal os vi | ...; 3*a*, col. 2: ⟦ Coplas dela | reyna de napoles. | ⟦ Emperatrizes y reynas | ...; 3*b*, in col. 2: ⟦ Villancico. | ⟦ No ay plazer eñsta vida | ...; 4*a*, in col. 1: Otro villancico | ⟦ Mal đ muchos no ɔsuela | ...; in col. 2: Coplas fechas | por rodrigo đ reynosa a vnas | serranas al tono del bayle del | villano. | ⟦ Mal encaramillo millo | ...

82. TORO (Álvaro de)
  ⟦ Disparates cōtrarios delos de | Iuan del enzina fechos por Aluaro de toro. |
  4°. [*]². [Sev., Crom., *c.* 1511–15.] (BNP)
  1*a*, col. 1: ⟦ Lleuaron vn combidado | ...

83. TORRES (Diego de)
  (P²)Ronostico o Iuyzio nue= | ua y sutilisamēte saca= | do por el muy Reuerēdo padre | fray Diego de tores dela orden | de sant Bernaldo doctor en ar= | tes y maestro en sacra theologia. Sacado de lo mas cier | to de toda la estrologia. Y va hasta el año de veynte y | cinco...

4°. [*]². Bordered title-page, with composite woodcut above title; woodcut on 2b. The prose prognostication printed in long lines. [Val., Cost., winter 1519|20.] (BNM)

2b, col. 1: Romāce del na | cimiento de nu | estro señor jesu cristo. | [woodcut] | ❲ Triste estaua el padre adā | ...

Facsimile by J. Sancho Rayón [Madrid, 187–]. The prognostication is for the years 1520–5. The Romance is by Torres Naharro.

# CHAPTER V

# *The Text of the Burgos Chap-book*

MR NORTON has proved that the Burgos chap-book, here reproduced in facsimile, was printed between 1515 and 1519. It contains six Spanish ballads (*romances*), only one of which, as far as we are aware, had been printed before the earlier of these two dates. The four quarto leaves contain, then, the earliest texts so far discovered of five ballads (in fact there are really six, because of a contamination in the text of no. iv), and of these one (no. ii) is known only in a single unique print, another (no. vi) has never been reprinted at all, and still another (no. i) was known only in a much shorter version. We furnish here for the attention of those interested in ballad texts and transmission five important texts that are not only valuable in themselves but also throw light on the early history of the *romancero*, so acutely discussed by Don Ramón Menéndez Pidal. I shall examine the versions one by one in the order in which they occur in the chap-book.

## (i) *Romançe de Amadis y Oriana*

The earliest known edition of *Los quatro libros de Amadís de Gaula* was printed at Saragossa by G. Coci in 1508.[1] The text was revised by Garci Rodríguez de Montalvo, who appears to have abbreviated by about one-third the text that was current during the first third of the fifteenth century, if the manuscript fragments, recovered some years ago by Don Antonio Rodríguez-Moñino,[2] from a portion of the third book, are a reliable guide. Ballads about Amadís and Oriana may perhaps antedate the printed book of 1508.

No one, to our knowledge, has reprinted the entire *Amadís romance* contained in the

[1] Norton, pp. 74, 164.
[2] 'El primer manuscrito del *Amadís de Gaula*. Noticia bibliográfica por Antonio Rodríguez-Moñino, seguida de Nota paleográfica sobre el manuscrito del Amadís por Agustín Millares Carlo, y El lenguaje del Amadís manuscrito por Rafael Lapesa.' Offprint from the Boletín de la Real Academia Española, XXXVI (1956), 199–225. See also: Edwin B. Place, '¿Montalvo autor o refundidor del *Amadís* IV y V?' *Homenaje a Rodríguez-Moñino* (Madrid, 1966), II, 77–80.

Cambridge chap-book. Neither Entwistle nor Menéndez Pidal mentions ballads about Amadís in the works I have consulted. Nevertheless Durán had earlier printed four, three of which were briefly mentioned by Sir Henry Thomas.[1] They begin:

(*a*) En la selua esta Amadis
el leal enamorado
tal vida estaua haziendo...[2]

(*b*) En la selua esta Amadis
el leal enamorado.
De lagrimas de sus ojos...[3]

(*c*) Despues q̃ el muy esforçado
Amadis q̃ fue de Gaula...[4]

(*d*) En vn hermoso vergel
de flores todo cercado...[5]

There is a fifth among the Prague chap-books:

(*e*) Amadis el muy famoso
hijo del buen rey de gaula...[6]

This is in fact a gloss of 22 lines of our *romance* by a poet named Quesada. The lines glossed are those corresponding to lines 1–16, 19–20, and 23–6 in our text, which has a total of 148 lines. The Prague chap-book appears to have been printed at Seville in 1540 or later. Our text is therefore earlier and much more complete.

[1] Durán, nos. 335–7 and 1890. Henry Thomas, *Spanish and Portuguese Romances of Chivalry* (Cambridge, 1920), p. 78.

[2] *Cancionero de Amberes*, fol. 263ʳ.

[3] *Pliegos*, Madrid, IV, no. CXLVI. ('Aqui comiença vna glosa al Romance de Amadis y es de saber que el romance es nueuo y la glosa assi mesmo nueua sentida y muy gentil segun q̃ por ella veres...' [Burgos, Juan de Junta, *c.* 1540].) British Museum: C.63.f.14. ('Aqui comiença vna glosa al Romance de Amadis. Con vna glosa ala mia gran pena forte'. [Burgos, Alonso de Melgar, *c.* 1525].)

[4] *Cancionero de Amberes*, fol. 263ᵛ. *Pliegos*, Praga, II, no. XLII. ('Romãce de dõ reynaldos d̃ Mõtaluan. Con vnas coplas de Juan del Enzina. Y vn romance de Amadis.' [Burgos, Felipe de Junta, 156–].) *Pliegos*, Madrid, II, no. LXXII. ('Romance del conde Alarcos: y dela infanta Solisa. Hecho por Pedro de Riaño. Y otro romãce de Amadis: q̃ dize...' [Toledo, ?*c.* 1540].) Bibliothèque Nationale, Paris. ('Romance del conde Alarcos τ la Infanta Solisa.

Fecho por Pedro de riaño. Otro Romãce de Amadis: q̃ dize...' [Seville, Jacobo Cromberger, *c.* 1520].) See *List of poetical chap-books*, no. 3. See also: E. M. Wilson, 'Some Spanish verse chap-books of the seventeenth century', *Transactions of the Cambridge Bibliographical Society*, III, 4 (1962), 327–34.

[5] *Pliegos*, Praga, II, no. XLIX. ('Glosa dela reyna Troyana y vn romance de Amadis: hecho por Alonso de Salaya, con otros romances y obras suyas.' [Burgos, Felipe de Junta, 156–].) *Pliegos*, Madrid, II, no. LIV. ('Romãce dela reyna Troyana glosado: y vn Romance de Amadis: hecho por Alonso de Salaya. Con dos romãces de Gayferos: enlos quales se cõtiene como mataron a don Galuan.' [Burgos, Juan de Junta, ?153–].)

[6] *Pliegos*, Praga, II, no. LIX. ('Aqui comiençan .iiij. Romances glosados: y este primero dize / caminaua el cauallero y otro que dize / Amadis el muy famoso. y otro que dize / Triste esta la gentil dama, y otro que dize / Enel tiempo q̃ me vi. Cõ vn mote glosado.' [Seville, mid-sixteenth century].)

The Cambridge text deals selectively and compactly with events described in the following chapters of the novel: I, xxi, xl, xlii; II, xliii–xlvi, xlviii–xlviiii, li–lii.[1] It refers to the events in the hero's life most popular with sixteenth-century readers: his disinterested love for Oriana, the dwarf's unfortunate misapprehension that his master had fallen in love with Briolanja, Oriana's jealousy and dismissal of Amadís, his abandonment of his squire and penance on the Peña Pobre, until the maiden of Denamarca brought him back to Great Britain, where he fought the giant Famongomadán and was reunited with Oriana. Those who read the novel will see that the ballad-author has missed out many battles and adventures, including all trace of Amadís's trials as a true lover on the Ínsula Firme. At times the narrative appears confused, notably in lines 13–18:

> mucho la queria amadis
> mas era amor de hermana
> vn enano de amadis
> al reues esto tomaua
> segun se querian los dos
> el amor los conquistaua

the 'la' in line 13 must refer to Princess Briolanja, so that the love Amadís bore her was that of a brother for a sister. The situation was wrongly interpreted by Ardián the dwarf, who assumed that the other kind of love had conquered both lovers and reported that fact to Oriana. Otherwise the narrative is clear and straightforward. At times the words of the novel are recalled in the *romance*:

> que se fuese do no lo viese (28)
>
> no parescays ante mí ni en parte donde yo
>     sea (II, xliiii, p. 370)
>
> andando por la espessura
> al pie de vna sierra agra
> hallaron vna gran fuente
> que tenia muy buen agua (43–6)

Vnos árboles que eran en vna ribera de vna agua que de la montaña descendía. (II, xlviii, p. 391) Se metió por lo más espesso de la montaña...Estonces entró en vna gran vega que al pie de vna montaña estaua, y en ella hauía dos árboles altos, que estaban sobre vna fuente; y fue allá por dar agua a su cauallo... (*ibid.* p. 393)

> τ los frenos escondiera
> en vna espessura mala (73–4)

Escondió la silla y el freno de Gandalín entre vnas espessas matas... (*ibid.* pp. 392–3)

[1] All references to the novel are taken from the edition in progress by Edwin B. Place, the first volume of which appeared in 1959.

There is no reason to think that this ballad antedates the printed edition of the *Amadís* of 1508. We find in it a good many traces of the traditional *romancero* phraseology:

> del buen rey de gaula
>
> jamas nunca lo dexaua
>
> llorando delos sus ojos
>
> dela su boca hablaua
>
> bien oyeres lo que fablara
>
> consolaos el mi señor

and so forth. This *romance* has not the merit of, say, the long Don Gaiferos ballad or that of *El Conde Alarcos*; but it illustrates the vitality of the minstrel ballads during the early sixteenth century, which could even absorb a cultivated novel as a source.

The Prague version, glossed by Quesada, neatly supports Don Ramón's generalizations about how the longer versions of a given ballad generally precede shorter ones (e.g. *El Conde Arnaldos*, *El prisionero* and 'Ya comienzan los franceses...'—see below). We may note that the lines I have called obscure have been smoothed away and that the fragment describes merely the heart of the situation: Amadís's fidelity, Oriana's stern command faithfully obeyed. There is no saying whether the poem had or had not lost its last 122 lines when Quesada heard it sung or saw a printed version of it. Possibly he had a complete text like ours and chose to gloss only the lines that he most liked. If so a single man—not the consensus of tradition—brought about the change in length. In other words, the *romance* may have been shortened because a poet intervened in its transmission, not because the taste of those who heard *romances* sung (or read them?) wanted an increased poetic concentration as the sixteenth century advanced. There are, however, too many unknown factors for us to be dogmatic in this single case.

Don Eugenio Asensio has suggested to me that this poem may provide a link between the novel and the *Tragicomedia de Amadís de Gaula* of Gil Vicente. Some of Vicente's divergences from the novel are common also to the ballad. In both ballad and play Oriana's change of heart is due to the account given her of Amadís's behaviour when he received her first letter. But the *romance* does not make the dwarf Ardián into a traitor to his master as did Vicente, and the events at the end of it (the battle with ten knights, the death of Famongomadán, etc.) have no place in the play.

## (ii) *Romance del rey Malsín*

A hundred-line-long fragment of a Spanish epic about the battle of Roncesvalles was printed by Don Ramón Menéndez Pidal in 1917.[1] It was discovered in Pamplona. It has since been studied by Entwistle, by Monsieur Horrent and by Don Ramón himself. Of this poem Entwistle remarked: 'It does not appear to have been older than the thirteenth century, since Reynaud of Montauban is as great a hero as Roland. The moment preserved is that in which Charlemagne returns to the field to scrutinize the dead.'[2] All three scholars agree that the *Romance de doña Alda*, the *Romance de la huída del rey Marsín* and its derivative which begins: 'Domingo era de ramos...' (see below) probably began as fragments of the lost epic. Don Ramón further noted that although the *Chanson de Roland* was popular in many parts of Europe in the thirteenth century, only in Spain did ballads originate about the fair Aude and king Marsilie.[3] Our ballad, then, is a development from a lost fragment of either the existing epic or of a poem like it.

In our poem the following epic characteristics appear:

1. The relation between Roldán and Renaldos appears to be similar to that which is found in the Pamplona fragment.

2. The scansion of the lines is irregular, though octosyllables predominate. The scansion of the *Roncesvalles* fragment is also irregular.

3. The assonance of our *romance* varies:

| | |
|---|---|
| á–(e) | lines 1–6 |
| a–a | lines 7–34 |
| á–(e) | lines 35–66 |
| í–(e) | lines 67–114 |

These irregular assonances may perhaps correspond to differing assonances in different *laisses* of the lost epic original. For these and other reasons Don Ramón looks on this ballad as one of the epic fragments that have undergone least change in the course of traditional transmission but, he adds, perhaps the long final denial of King Marsín may be a later lyric outburst to make sure that the final victory was for the French.[4] The Cambridge chap-book version does not contradict this opinion.

---

[1] '*Roncesvalles*, un nuevo cantar de gesta del siglo XIII', *Revista de Filología Española*, IV (1917), 105–204.

[2] Entwistle, pp. 172–3. See also p. 102.

[3] *Romancero hispánico*, I, 188 and 247.

[4] *Romancero hispánico*, loc. cit.

Hitherto the *romance*, which begins 'Ya comienzan los franceses...', has been known only in a single text, contained in a chap-book preserved at the Biblioteca Nacional, Madrid, almost certainly printed by Juan de Junta of Burgos, probably in about 1535 and certainly not before 1527.[1] It was first reprinted by Menéndez y Pelayo; more recently it has been carefully copied by Monsieur Horrent and by Don Antonio Rodríguez-Moñino.[2] Our text is certainly earlier than the one at Madrid, for which it could, conceivably, have provided a copy text. In any case the place of printing of both editions of the poem is the same, so there is probably a more or less direct relation between them. A comparison of variants may help to settle the question.

Here is a list of the most important variants between the two texts:

| LINE | CAMBRIDGE TEXT | MADRID TEXT |
|------|----------------|-------------|
| 5 | alli fablo baldoninos [*sic*] | alli hablo baldouinos |
| 6 | bien oyereys lo que dira | bien oyreys lo que dira |
| 9 | mas de sed que no hambre | mas de sed que no de hãbre |
| 10 | a dios quiero dar el alma | a dios quiero yo dar el alma |
| 14 | que vna vez el cuerno tanga | que vna vez el cuerno taña |
| 16 | questa enlos puertos daspa | questa enlos puertos despaña |
| 22 | que yo rogado me estaua | que ya rogado mestaua |
| 23 | mas rogadlo a dõ renaldos | mas rogaldo a don renaldos |
| 37 | por tã pocos moros como estos | q̃ atã pocos moros como estos |
| 51 | Alli salio vn moro perro | alli salio vn perro moro |
| 56 | ysles huyendo delante | ysles fuyendo delante |
| 57 | o mal aya el rey malsin | o mal aya el rey marsin |
| 58 | que sueldo os manda dar | que soldada os manda dare |
| 60 | que vos lo manda pagar | que vos la manda pagare |
| 62 | que las venis a ganar | que la venis a ganare |
| 65 | y a bueltas τ rebueltas | y bueltas y rebueltas |
| 66 | los franceses huyendo van | los franceses fuyendo van |
| 78 | huyendo va el rey malsin | fuyendo va el rey marsin |
| 83 | las vozes que yua dando | las bozes quel yua dando |
| 90 | la cabeça de oro te hize | la cabeça de oro te hiz |
| 92 | offrecillos yo a ti | ofrecilos yo a ti |
| 100 | mahoma no lo traygo aqui | mahoma no lo trayo aqui |
| 109 | esse me bautizara | esse me baptizara |
| 113 | que yrme quiero a roma | que yr no quiero a roma |

[1] *Pliegos*, Madrid, I, no. XVII, 125–32.
[2] Marcelino Menéndez y Pelayo, *Antología de poetas líricos castellanos*, X (1923), 245. Jules Horrent, *Roncesvalles—Étude sur le fragment de cantar de gesta conservé à l'Archivo de Navarra (Pampelune)*, Paris, 1951, pp. 219–22. A. Rodríguez-Moñino, *Cancionerillos góticos castellanos*, Valencia, 1954, pp. 74–8.

I have not included among the variants the replacements of the early ampersands by the ordinary conjunction 'y', nor have I noted purely orthographic changes. There are occasional archaisms (paragogic 'e's, 'f' for modern Spanish 'h', etc.) which occur in the later text but not in the earlier; this may mean that the Madrid version derives from an earlier print than the Cambridge one. The form 'Marsín' is nearer to the original Marsilie than is the Cambridge chap-book's 'Malsin'. Nevertheless some Cambridge readings seem older than those from Madrid: the changes that have occurred in lines 6, 9, 16, 58, 83 seem all to have been made to make irregular lines more regular. But we must be cautious here. In line 16 the 'puertos daspa' seem mysterious, and Don Ramón reminds us that the 'puertos de España' is a French phrase which occurs twice in the Oxford manuscript of the *Chanson de Roland* (lines 824, 1152).[1] There is, however, a French river Aspe which flows through Oloron and joins the Gave de Pau; the 'Puertos de Aspa' might then stand for the pass over the Pyrenees via Canfranc. Moreover Dr Peter Rickard has brought to my notice the following lines in the French epic of *Girart de Roussillon*:

> De Alemaigne en Provence, les regorsz,
> Des Mongiu tros qu'en Aspre, d'andoz les porz,
> I viennent li baron, c'uns ne s'en torz.[2]

And in *La Chanson de Floovant*:

> Il ne ait si vailant de ci que au por d'Apre.[3] (line 1609)

Don Ramón also tells us that in early Spanish the plural form was often used to describe a mountain pass and that 'los puertos de Aspa' was the common name for what is now Somport, the pass of Canfranc.[4] So if we allow that 'Apre' = 'Aspre' = 'Aspe' = 'Aspa', then perhaps the 'puertos de Aspa' of our text may—given the geographical inaccuracy that might be expected from the transmitters of ballads—represent as legitimate a reading as the 'Puertos de España' of the later text. In other places there is a good deal to be said for the more modern Madrid readings; no one can doubt that the penultimate line makes better sense in the Madrid text than in the Cambridge one. Here again the more modern reading may in fact represent that of a much earlier one.

[1] R. Menéndez Pidal, *La Chanson de Roland y el neotradicionalismo* (Madrid, 1959), p. 401.

[2] Ed. W. M. Hackett, Société des Anciens Textes Français, lines 2354–6.

[3] Ed. F. H. Bateson, Société des Anciens Textes Français, line 1609.

[4] R. Menéndez Pidal, *La Chanson...*, p. 213.

There must have been other prints of this *romance* which have disappeared without leaving a trace behind them. As both our texts come from Burgos, as both of them consist of 114 lines, as many of the differences between them are unimportant, and as many lines (including some irregular ones) are identical in the two editions, we are driven to the conclusion that both printers followed lost earlier texts. Nevertheless the two variants that we have just examined imply that the transmission of the ballad may have been influenced by some diverging readings from the old epic. To a singer near Burgos the 'Puertos de Aspa' and the 'Puertos de España' could easily have become confused, and a later printer, who remembered fragments of an oral version, might well introduce occasional details from memory into the text he was setting up from a printed copy, whether he was conscious that he was doing so or not. So there may be traces of oral tradition in the variants that we have looked at, even though the printer was set to make a copy of a lost printed version.

The theory that this ballad is at bottom a fragment of the Spanish *Roncesvalles* fits all the facts. Don Ramón, in a passage already referred to, remarks that its style is epic or epic-lyric, except for the conclusion. He uses adjectives like 'precioso' and 'extraordinario' to describe it, and this ballad must be allowed as one of the greatest poems in the whole traditional *romancero*. To point out all its merits would insult our readers. I mention only the words of Roldán and Renaldos at the beginning and the vivid similes that describe Renaldos's ferocity in the battle.

The last lines of this ballad—from the line 'los franceses huyendo van...' to the end—became separated from the rest and grew into a shorter lyrical ballad which has a new opening: 'Domingo era de ramos...' This version was reprinted in many standard collections,[1] and thanks perhaps to a gloss by one Gonzalo de Montalbán (or Montalbo) was printed at least seven times during the sixteenth century.

1. *Cancionero de Amberes*, Antwerp, 1547-8, fol. 229.
2. *Pliegos*, Madrid, II, no. LXIX, probably of Toledo, *c.* 1540.
3. *Pliegos*, Madrid, III, no. CXV, probably of Burgos, by Felipe de Junta, 1560-70.
4. *Pliegos*, Praga, I, no. XXIV, probably of Burgos, Felipe de Junta, end of sixteenth century.
5. *Pliegos*, Praga, II, no. LXI, probably of Burgos, Juan or Felipe de Junta, *c.* 1545.
6. Cracow, no. 84, 'Impresso en Granada en casa de Hugo de Mena. Año de 1573'.[2]
7. *Pliegos*, Praga, II, no. LXIV, place and date unidentified, probably after 1550.

[1] Wolf and Hofmann; Durán, I, no. 394, p. 262; etc.
[2] E. Porębowicz, 'Zbiór nieznanych hiszpańskich ulotnych druków znajdujących się w Bibljotece Jagiellońskiej w Krakowie', *Rozprawy i Sprawozdania z Posiedzeń wydziału Filologicznego Akademii Umiejętności*, XV (1891), 252-319.

I print below what appears to be the earliest known text—no. 2; I italicize the changes made from the longer poem (*Romance del rey Marsín*); opposite each line are the variants from the other versions that were accessible.

| | |
|---|---|
| *Domingo era de ramos* | |
| *la passion quieren dezir* | |
| *quando moros ⁊ christianos* | |
| *todos entran enla lid* | |
| *ya desmayan* los franceses | |
| *ya comiençan de huyr* | |
| *o quan* bien los esforçaua | |
| *este* roldan paladin | esse [*all other texts*] |
| buelta buelta los franceses | |
| con coraçon ala lid | |
| mas vale morir *por buenos* | |
| que *desonrados* viuir | |
| ya boluian los franceses | |
| con coraçon ala lid | |
| *a los encuentros primeros* | primeros encuentros—4, 7. |
| *mataron sexenta* [*sic*] *mil* | ses(s)enta [*all other texts*] |
| por *las sierras dalta mira* | |
| huyendo va el rey marsin | Marsil—3. |
| cauallero en vna zebra | |
| no por mengua de rosin [*sic*] | falta—3; rocin [*all other texts*] |
| la sangre que del *corria* | salia—4. |
| las yeruas haz *en* [*sic*] teñir | haze—1, 4, 7; hazia—3; quiree [*sic*]—5. |
| las bozes que yua dando | quel—5, 7; que el—3. |
| al cielo quieren subir | |
| reniego de ti mahoma | |
| y de quanto hizo [*sic*] enti | hize [*all other texts*] |
| hize te cuerpo de plata | |
| pies y manos de *vn* marfil | de marfil—3, 4, 5. |
| *hize te casa de meca* | |
| *donde adorassen enti* | |
| ⁊ por mas te honrar mahoma | por mas—3. |
| cabeça de oro te fiz | hize—4. |
| sesenta mil caualleros | |
| ati te los offreci | |
| mi muger *la reyna* mora | Abrayma—4. |
| te offreciera treynta mil | ofrecio—1. |

The losses from the old ballad are serious, though a good deal survives. The revision has added very little to the literary merit of the surviving lines; it remains interesting as a symptom of ballad history, but no more. Two details of collation show traces of the survival of parts of the earlier text: the corría/salía of line 21 and the la reyna mora/Abrayma of the penultimate line. Curiously these both occur in what—for typographical reasons—we consider to be one of the later texts. Other changes have been commented on by Don Ramón.[1]

The line 'Reniego de ti Mahoma' antedates the existing versions of both ballads. In the *Cancionero general* of Valencia, 1511, we find among the *romances*: 'Otro [romance] del mismo [Diego de] san pedro trocado por el q̃ dize reniego de ti mahomad.' It begins:

Reniego de ti amor
y de quãto te serui...[2]

The poem appeared in various later editions of the *Cancionero*, as well as in the *Cancionero de romances sin año* during the sixteenth century. Later the phrase became proverbial.[3] Could it go back to the thirteenth-century epic?

### (iii) *Romance de Gayferos*

This *romance* is not the famous poem about Don Gayferos's escape with the beautiful Melisendra from the city of Sansueña,[4] nor is it concerned with how the young Gayferos was saved from the cruelty of Galván.[5] The claim of Charles Nodier that this Cambridge chap-book is a 'source de Don Quichotte'[6] has nothing to support it but the name of Don Gayferos; this poem throws no light on chapters XXV–XXVII of the Second Part of *Don Quixote*. It simply recounts how a Christian prince escapes by himself from a Moorish prison and a Moorish city. The possible links that this story may have with the adventures of Walter of Aquitaine were mooted by Entwistle and discussed with much learning by Don Ramón.[7] This is the fourth ballad of Don Gayferos mentioned by Entwistle, of which he said: 'Gayferos...is

[1] *Romancero hispánico*, I, 248.
[2] See the facsimile edition edited by Antonio Rodríguez-Moñino and published by the Spanish Academy in 1958, fol. cxxxiij^v.
[3] E. M. Wilson and J. Sage, *Poesías líricas en las obras dramáticas de Calderón—citas y glosas* (London, 1964), no. 112, p. 90.
[4] Thomas, *Early*, III. *Romance de don Gayferos*, printed by J. Cromberger, Seville, c. 1515... Cambridge, 1927. Also Durán, no. 377.
[5] Durán, nos. 374, 375.
[6] '[Ici] se trouve la fameuse romance de Gayferos, à jamais célèbre par un des chapitres les plus piquants de Don Quichotte.' (See Chapter I, note 2.)
[7] Entwistle, pp. 97, 177. *Romancero hispánico*, I, 286–300.

escaping from prison [by himself]... This is somewhat incoherent, and belongs to the traditions of Walter.' The link seems tenuous to the point of invisibility.

The only other known text of this ballad is contained in the collection at Prague,[1] where it is called 'El romance de Gayferos'. We have not been able to identify the printer, place of printing or date of it, but perhaps it came out in the middle years of the century. The variants have some interest:

| LINES | CAMBRIDGE | PRAGUE |
|---|---|---|
| 1–2 | Media noche era passada | Media noche era porfilo |
|  | y otra media por passar | los gallos queriã cãtar |
| 4–7 | salio de cautiuidad | salio de captiuidad |
|  | muerto dexa el carcellero | muerto dexa al carcelero |
|  | y quantos conel estan | y a quantos conel estan |
|  | vase por vna calle abaxo | vase por vna calle ayuso |
| 10 | como aquel que la bien sabe | como aquel que bien la sabe |
| 14 | no falla por do andar | no halla por do botar |
| 21–2 | alli fablara el moro | alli hablara el moro |
|  | bien oyres lo que dira | bien oyreys lo que dira |
| 24–8 | cartas lleuas de mensaje | y cartas lleuas de mensaje |
|  | esperasses tu al lalua | esperasses tu al dia |
|  | con los otros saliras | y con los otros saldras |
|  | De questo oyera gayferos | desque esto oyera Gayferos |
|  | bien oyeres lo que dira | bien oyreys lo que dira |
| 35 | oydo lo ha vna morica | oydo lo auia vna morica |
| 38 | y empeçole de hablar | empeçole de hablar |
| 41 | la muger tenias moça | la muger tienes moça |
| 43 | de que esto oyo el moro | desque esto oyo el moro |
| 51 | muerto cayo el moro | muerto cae el morico |
| 53–4 | de que esto vio la morica | desque esto vio la morica |
|  | empeço de gritos dar | empieça de gritos dar |
| 60 | ya estaua en libertad | ya estaua enla christindad. |

The study of these variants leads me to think that probably there was little part played by oral transmission between them. The contamination of the two opening lines by those of the *Romance del conde Claros* (Media noche era por filo / los gallos querian cantar) might easily be due to a compositor who thought those well-known lines more elegant. The change in the last line might well be a similar 'bright idea' to improve the scansion. The other alterations seem largely due to the wish to remove archaisms (*carcellero, oyres, saliras*...) or to try to rationalize tenses. Possibly, though,

---

[1] *Pliegos*, Praga, II, no. XLI. Reprinted by Wolf and Hofmann, no. 174, II, 248.

the substitution of 'botar' for 'andar' may be an oral change. Otherwise we have to do here with the kind of variants made by a printer who wants to make an old text more up to date in language and in style.

The Cambridge text is certainly older than the Prague one. It bears some resemblance to other *romances*, notably that fine *Romance de Morayma* from the *Cancionero general*,[1] reprinted in other sixteenth-century collections. There we find:

> hablome en algarauia
> como aquel que la bien sabe
>
> abras me las puertas mora
> si ala te guarde de mal
>
> quando esto oy cuytada
> comenceme a leuantar
>
> y abrila de par en par.

Other ballad clichés abound in it. Our ballad lacks the magnificent concentration of *Morayma*, but it is not to be shrugged aside. Gayferos's falsehoods and murders need no justification from the point of view of the singer, but their effect is well brought out by the conversation of the gate-keeper with the girl and her final cries of grief. We learn that men whose lives are at stake must be ruthless, but we learn also the human cost of their ruthlessness.

(iv) *Romance fecho ala muerte de don Pedro Caruajal y de don Alonso su hermano*

There were two different traditions about the story of King Ferdinand IV's unjust condemnation of the brothers Carvajal (or Caravajal) and of how they summoned him to answer for it before Almighty God. According to the more learned writers, beginning with the *Crónica de Fernando IV*, an unnamed gentleman was unjustly punished for the murder of a Juan Alonso de Benavides. The shorter redaction of the *Crónica de Alfonso onceno* repeated this story. The *Valerio de las historias* of 1487 calls the murdered man Gómez de Benavides and the wrongly punished brothers Pedro and Juan Alonso de Carabajal. Zurita, Argote de Molina and Mariana repeated the legend but changed the brothers' Christian names: Zurita called them Pedro and Alonso; Argote and Mariana called them Pedro and Juan. Lope de Vega's play, *La inocente sangre* (probably written between 1604 and 1608) follows these last

---

[1] *Ed. cit.*, fol. cxxxv*.

writers: the murdered man's name is Gómez, the brothers' Pedro and Juan.[1] The more popular tradition names the Carvajales, but omits any mention of Benavides. The brothers were here accused of various crimes against the peasantry, not of the murder of a nobleman. This is the account given in the three surviving *romances*, which, strangely enough, Lope did not use in his stirring, if irregular, *comedia*.

The ballad in the Cambridge chap-book is known in two later versions as the *Romance del rey don Fernando que dizen que murió aplazado* or as the *Romance del rey don Fernando quarto*.[2] There is of course no historical evidence that King Ferdinand IV of Castile died suddenly because he was summoned to the judgement of God by the brothers Carvajal whom he had unjustly sentenced to a cruel death exactly thirty days before. Nevertheless such a story was current within thirty years of his death in 1312, for it was vaguely related in the chronicle of his reign written *c.* 1340, though there is no sign of it in the redaction of the *Crónica general* of 1344. The brothers were accused in Martos of having murdered Juan Alonso de Benavides; before they were executed they cited the king to appear before God within thirty days; the king went to Jaén, where he died suddenly, exactly thirty days later, during a siesta. Don Ramón supposes that the *Crónica de Fernando IV* incorporated the story as told in an oral ballad, which, however, was not known to the compiler of 1344.[3] If this is so the poem is one of the earliest news ballads (*romances noticiosos*) composed to commemorate events of the immediate past.

Don Ramón tells us also how the ballad was well known in the fifteenth century. The most important testimony is that of Juan de Mena in his *El labirintho*:

> Yredes a sancho tercero callando
> Aquel que la fuerte tarifa conquiso
> Yra ya dexando de ver vuestro viso
> Todos los hechos del tercer(o) fernando
> Aquel que alcaudete gano batallando
> Del qual se dize morir emplazado
> Delos que de martos ouo despeñado
> Según dizen rusticos deste cantando.[4]

---

[1] Marcelino Menéndez y Pelayo, *Estudios sobre el teatro de Lope de Vega* (Madrid, 1923), IV, 271–83. Lope's play, first printed in his *Parte XIX* of 1623, can be found in volume IX of the Academy edition and in volume LII of the Biblioteca de Autores Españoles.

[2] See Wolf and Hofmann, no. 64, I, 201; Durán, II, no. 960.

[3] *Romancero hispánico*, I, 310–11.

[4] Facsimile of the edition of Seville, 1496, edited by Don Antonio Pérez Gómez, Valencia, 1955, fol. f, ij<sup>v</sup>.

(Presumably Mena called Ferdinand IV the III because Ferdinand II was king only of León, not of Castile.) These words clearly prove that ballads about King Ferdinand the Summoned were current in Castile while Mena was writing his ambitious allegorical poem; he finished it in February, 1444.[1] We are also told that Isabel the Catholic often listened to the ballad to remind her of the dangers of royal injustice.[2] The buffoon of Charles V, Francesillo de Zúñiga, who died in 1532, refers in his burlesque chronicle to a lost *romance* that begins: 'En Martos estaba el rey...' which, as Don Ramón acutely perceived, probably refers to a version of this poem.[3] In 1550 Lorenzo de Sepúlveda published a learned ballad, which closely follows the chronicles, about the same affair. It begins: 'A don Pedro y don Alonso...' and may be found in Durán.[4]

The two later versions of our *romance* occur in the *Cancionero de Amberes* and in one of the Spanish verse chap-books at Prague.[5] The latter was probably printed by Felipe de Junta of Burgos in 1550 or perhaps later. Although the *Cancionero de Amberes* antedates the chap-book, the latter version seems to give the earlier text.[6] Both these later versions (but not the Cambridge text) begin with verses praising the religious practices of the king; Don Ramón points out that these lines differ in assonance from the remainder of the ballad and go against its intention.[7] He supposes that these lines referred originally to Ferdinand III, 'Fernando el Santo', and became associated with our poem through the confusions of an ignorant singer. As will soon be seen the Cambridge text also is contaminated—by a different ballad about another King Ferdinand—and this fact makes Don Ramón's theory all the more probable. Here are the three texts in parallel columns:

| CAMBRIDGE | PRAGUE | ANTWERP |
|---|---|---|
| | Valame nuestra señora | Valas me nuestra señora |
| | que dizen de la ribera | qual dizen de la ribera |
| | dõde el buẽ rey don fernãdo | donde el buen rey don Feruando [*sic*] |
| | tuuo la su quarentena | tuuo la su quarentena |
| | desde el miercoles coruillo | desdel miercoles coruillo |
| | hasta el jueues de la cena | hasta el jueues de la cena |

[1] *Romancero hispánico*, II, 26.
[2] *Ibid.*
[3] *Ibid.* p. 184.
[4] Durán, no. 961. *Romances Nueuamente sacados de historias antiguas dela cronica de España* compuestos por Lorenço de Sepulveda... Antwerp, 1551, fol. 79ʳ.

[5] Facsimile edition, fol. 165ʳ. *Pliegos*, Praga, I, no. XXXIX.
[6] J. F. Peeters Fontainas, *L'Officine espagnole de Martin Nutius à Anvers*, Antwerp, 1956 (no. 22, p. 42), assigns the date 1547/8 to the *Cancionero de romances*.
[7] *Romancero hispánico*, I, 311–12.

# THE TEXT OF THE BURGOS CHAP-BOOK

| CAMBRIDGE | PRAGUE | ANTWERP |
|---|---|---|
| | el Rey no afeyto su barba | quel rey no hizo la barba |
| | ni si lauo la cabeça | ni peyno la su cabeça |
| | vna silla era su cama | vna silla era su cama |
| | vn canto su cabecera | vn canto por cabecera |
| | quarenta pobres comian | los quarenta pobres comen |
| | cada dia a la su mesa | cada dia ala su mesa |
| | de lo que a los pobres sobra | de lo que alos pobres sobra |
| | el Rey hazia su cena | el rey haze la su cena |
| | con vara de oro en mano | con vara de oro en su mano |
| | bien haze seruir su mesa | bien haze seruir la mesa |
| | dizen le sus caualleros | dizen le sus caualleros |
| | do hauia de tener la fiesta | donde iras tener la fiesta |
| | a Jaen dize señores | a jaen dize señores |
| | con mi señora la Reyna | con mi señora la reyna |
| En jaen esta el buen rey | | |
| esse buen rey don fernando | | |
| en jaen tuuo la pascua | en Jaen tuuo la pascua | despues que estuuo en jaen |
| y en martos el cabo daño | y en Martos el cabodaño | y la fiesta ouo passado |
| τ vase para alcaudete | partese para Alcaudete | partese para alcaudete |
| esse castillo nombrado | esse castillo nombrado | esse castillo nombrado |
| los pies tiene enel estribo | el pie tiene en el estribo | el pie tiene en el estriuo |
| que no ha descaualgado | aun no hauia descaualgado | que aun no se auia apeado |
| quando le dauan querella | quando le dauan querella | quando le dauan querella |
| daquesos dos hijos dalgo | de dos hombres hijos dalgo | de dos hombres hijos dalgo |
| | y dauan le la querella | τ la querella le dauan |
| | dos hombres como villanos | dos hombres como villanos |
| | | abarcas traen calçadas |
| | | τ aguijadas enlas manos |
| | justicia justicia el Rey | Justicia justicia rey |
| | pues que somos tus vassallos | pues que somos tus vasallos |
| de don pedro caruajal | de don Pedro Carauajal | de don Pedro carabajal |
| τ don alonso su hermano | y don Rodrigo su hermano | τ de don Alonso su hermano |
| que le robauan la tierra | q̃ nos corren nuestras tierras | que nos corren nuestras tierras |
| y le corrian el campo | y nos roban nuestro campo | τ nos robauan el campo |
| que le fuerçan las donzellas | fuerçã nos nuestras mugeres | τ nos fuerçan las mugeres |
| a tuerto τ a sin guisado | a tuerto y desaguisado | a tuerto τ desaguisado |
| | y comen nos la ceuada | comian nos la ceuada |
| | no nos la quieren pagar | sin despues querer pagallo |
| | hazen otras desuerguenças | hasen otras desuerguenças |

| CAMBRIDGE | PRAGUE | ANTWERP |
|---|---|---|
| | que era verguença contallo | que verguença era contallo |
| | Yo hare dellos justicia | yo hare dello justicia |
| | tornaos a vuestro ganado | tornaos a vuestro ganado |
| manda los prender el rey | manda pregonar el rey | manda a pregonar el rey |
| τ poner a buen recaudo | y por todo su reynado | τ por todo su reynado |
| | q̃ qualquier que los hallase | de qualquier que lo hallase |
| | le darian buen hallazgo | le daria buen hallazgo |
| | hallolos el Almirante | hallo los el almirante |
| | alla en Medina del campo | alla en medina del campo |
| | comprãdo muy ricas armas | comprando muy ricas armas |
| | jaezes para sus cauallos | jaezes para cauallos |
| | para yr a ver el pregon | |
| | que el buen Rey auia dado | |
| | Presos presos caualleros | presos presos caualleros |
| | presos presos hijos dalgo | presos presos hijos dalgo |
| | no por vos el Almirante | no por vos el almirante |
| | si de otro no es mandado | si de otro no traeys mandado |
| | sed presos los caualleros | estad presos caualleros |
| | que del Rey traygo mãdado | que del rey traygo recaudo |
| | Pues assi es el Almirante | plaze nos el almirante |
| | plaze nos de muy buẽ grado | por complir el su mandado |
| | por las sus jornadas ciertas | por las sus jornadas ciertas |
| | a Jaen hauian llegado | en jaen auian entrado |
| | mantenga te Dios el Rey | mantengate dios el rey |
| | mal vengades hijos dalgo | mal vengades hijos dalgo |
| mandales cortar los pies | mando les cortar los pies | manda les cortar los pies |
| mandales cortar los manos [sic] | mando les cortar las manos | manda les cortar las manos |
| mandaualos despeñar | y mandolos despeñar | τ manda los despeñar |
| de aquessa peña de martos | de aquella peña de Martos | de aquella peña de martos |
| o dela sierra de ayllo | | |
| porque caygan de mas alto | | |
| alli fablo el menor dellos | alli hablo el menordellos | ay hablara el vno dellos |
| que era mas acostumbrado | el menor y mas osado | el menor τ mas osado |
| | porque nos matas el Rey | porque lo hazes el rey |
| | siendo tan mal informado | porque hazes tal mandado |
| emplazamos te el buen rey | pues quexamonos de ti | querellamonos el rey |
| para ante el rey delo alto | al juez que es soberano | para ante el soberano |
| que de oy en treynta dias | que dentro de treynta dias | que dentro de treynta dias |
| que tu ayas de yr al plazo | con nosotros seas en plazo | vays con nosotros a plazo |
| oy cũples los veynte τ nueue | | |

| CAMBRIDGE | PRAGUE | ANTWERP |
|---|---|---|
| de mañana has dir al plazo | | |
| | y ponemos por testigos | τ ponemos por testigos |
| | a sanct Pedro y a sanct pablo | a san Pedro τ a san Pablo |
| | ponemos por testimonio | ponemos por escriuano |
| | al apostol Sanctiago | al apostol santiago |
| | τ sin mas poder dezir | el rey no mirando enello |
| | mueren estos hijos dalgo | hizo cumplir su mandado |
| | | por la falsa informacion |
| | | que los villanos le han dado |
| | | y muertos los caruajales |
| | | que lo auian emplazado |
| ellos en aquesto estando | | |
| estas palabras hablando | | |
| dio al rey vna maletia | antes de los treynta dias | antes de los treynta dias |
| quasi dolor de costado | malo esta el Rey dõ fernãdo | el se fallara muy malo |
| o que mal doliente haze [sic] | | |
| esse buen rey don fernando | | |
| los pies tiene cara oriente | el cuerpo cara oriente | |
| y la candela enla mano | y la candela enla mano | |
| a sus fijos todos quatro | | |
| a su cabecera tiene | | |
| τ los tres eran ligitimos | | |
| el otro era bastardo | | |
| esse que bastardo era | | |
| quedaua mejor librado | | |
| arçobispo de toledo | | |
| y enlas españas primado | | |
| si yo no muriera fijo | | |
| yo os llegara a padre santo | | |
| mas cõla renta q̃ os queda | | |
| bien podreys hijo alcançallo | | |
| τ acabada esta razon | | y desque fueron cumplidos |
| el alma a dios hauia dado | | en el postrer dia del plazo |
| asi murio este buen rey | assi fallescio su alteza | fue muerto dentro en leon [sic] |
| porla sententia q̃ auia dado. | desta manera citado. | do la sentencia ouo dado. |

The versions referred to as Prague and Antwerp contain much common material. Don Ramón has said that 'La versión del *Cancionero* [*de Amberes*] parece recuerdo tocado de la del pliego suelto [de Praga].'[1] The variants are mostly verbal such as

[1] In his prologue to the facsimile edition of the *Cancionero de Amberes*, p. xxv.

might have been made by a compositor from a corrected copy of an earlier printing of the Prague chap-book. There are some passages, though, in which oral variation occurs. The lines:

> abarcas traen calçadas
> aguijadas enlas manos

seem genuine enough, but they occur only in the corrected version. There may be other oral variants between these two versions. At the end of the poem, after the line 'antes de los treynta dias' the two texts diverge. Perhaps the last lines had been torn away at some stage of transmission, and a printer had to cope as best he could to finish the poem off. Here the *Cancionero* gives a less lame ending; it is also close to that in the Cambridge chap-book. If my theory is right the imperfect copy text lies behind the Prague text, but not behind the other two.

As in the more learned tradition, there are inconsistencies in the Christian names of the two brothers: Pedro and Rodrigo in the Prague chap-book, Pedro and Alonso in the Cambridge one, in the *Cancionero de Amberes* and in Sepúlveda. Both the later texts are contaminated by the account of the pious practices of (presumably) King Ferdinand III, but the Cambridge text has no such reference. We have not enough evidence to indicate when the contamination first took place.

> En jaen esta el buen rey
> esse buen rey don fernando

So begins the Cambridge text; the lost version quoted by Zúñiga began 'En Martos estaba el rey'. Ferdinand spent Easter in Jaén and finished the anniversary in Martos. After this the narrative moves more swiftly than in the later texts; the supposed misdeeds of the Carvajales are briefly told; nothing is said of their arrest by the Almirante. The king pronounces his savage sentence; the younger Carvajal summons him to appear before Almighty God within thirty days. After this come some confused lines, which may well indicate purely oral corruption; we are not even told that the brothers were executed! Following this is the description of Ferdinand's death, which is in fact—up to within four lines of the end of the poem—an interpolation of the *Romance del rey don Fernando primero*. The early part of the Cambridge text is greatly abbreviated; the later corrupted and expanded. The divergences in the first half may be due to the fact that there were about the year 1500 at least two patterns of narrative in circulation, of which one was more detailed than the other; the more detailed pattern then or later incorporated an account of the austerities of another

King Ferdinand. Don Ramón has proved that in many cases longer versions of a given ballad preceded shorter ones during the Spanish sixteenth century; the *Romance fecho ala muerte de don Pedro Carvajal y de don Alonso su hermano* cannot be proved to reverse this order.

The last lines of the Cambridge text are contaminated by the ballad about King Ferdinand I's death-bed. The *Romance del rey don Fernando primero*, which begins with the line: 'Doliente estaua doliente' was printed in the *Cancionero de Amberes*, and the *Romance de doña Vrraca* immediately followed it.[1] The two ballads differ in assonance, but the compiler of the *Silva de varios romances* of Saragossa, 1550, joined them together as a single poem.[2] Our chap-book contains only a part of the ballad of Ferdinand I, so we can disregard Doña Urraca's urgent pleas and immoral threats. This poem tells how when Ferdinand I lay dying he had beside him his three lawful and one illegitimate sons, to whom he turned and said that he regretted that he was going to die, because he had hoped to raise his bastard from being merely the Archbishop of Toledo to make him pope; nevertheless the king hoped that there was sufficient money left to him to enable him to do so. The death-bed of Ferdinand I was described in the *Crónica de veinte reyes*, where we are told that the bastard son who became archbishop was a figment in the imagination of the minstrels. The passage is interesting enough to be quoted:

Algunos dizen en sus cantares que avia el rey don Ferrando un fijo de ganançia que era cardenal en Roma, e legado de toda España, e abad de sant Fagunde, e arçobispo de Santiago, e prior de Monte Aragon; este fue el que poblo Arvas e avia nombre don Ferrando, mas esto non lo fallamos en las estorias de los maestros que las escripturas conpusieron, e por ende tenemos que no fue verdat, ca sy quier non es derecho que un omne tantas dignidades toviese. Este don Ferrando quando supo quel rey don Fernando su padre yazia mal doliente, allego grandes compañas de omes buenos...e vinose para el padre quanto mas ayna pudo. El rey don Ferrando amaua mucho a este cardenal e plogole con el quando lo vio.[3]

When, therefore, Don Ramón identifies this poem (in the version printed in the *Cancionero de Amberes*) as a derivative of a lost epic about the death of Ferdinand I of Castile, there seems every reason to accept his argument.[4] Thanks to the Cambridge chap-book we can now take this *romance* back another twenty years or so. When Don Ramón edited the *Cancionero de Amberes* in 1945, no earlier text than that he

[1] *Ed. cit.*, fols. 157ᵛ and 158ᵛ.
[2] *Romancero hispánico*, I, 208. Wolf and Hofmann, no. 35, I, 113, 114. Durán, 762. Carola Reig, *El cantar de Sancho II y cerco de Zamora* (Madrid, 1947), pp. 265–6.
[3] R. Menéndez Pidal, *Reliquias de la poesía épica española* (Madrid, 1951), pp. 242–3.
[4] *Romancero hispánico*, I, 205–7, 215.

edited was known; he then thought that the compiler of the *Cancionero* had probably taken his text from oral tradition.[1] The parallel texts that follow show that almost certainly a similar version had been in print for at least twenty years.

| CAMBRIDGE | ANTWERP |
|---|---|
| Romance fecho ala muerte de don Pedro caruajal y de don Alonso su hermano. (lines 37–52) | Romance del Rey don Fernando primero. |

| | |
|---|---|
| o que mal doliente haze [*sic*] | *Doliente estaua* doliente |
| esse buen rey don fernando | esse buen rey don Fernãdo |
| los pies tiene cara oriente | los pies tiene cara oriente |
| y la candela enla mano | y la candela enla mano |
| a sus fijos todos quatro | a*la* cabecera tiene |
| a su cabecera tiene | *los* sus fijos todos quatro |
| ⁊ los tres eran ligitimos | los tres eran *dela reyna* |
| el otro era bastardo | *y el vno* era bastardo |
| esse que bastardo era | ese que bastardo era |
| quedaua mejor librado | quedaua mejor librado |
| arçobispo de toledo | arçobispo *es* de Toledo |
| y enlas españas primado | y enlas españas *perlado* |
| si yo no muriera fijo | si yo no muriera *hijo* |
| yo os llegara a padre santo | *vos fuerades* padre santo |
| mas cõla renta q̃ os queda | mas con la renta que os queda |
| bien podreys hijo alcançallo | bien podreys hijo alcançarlo. |

Traces of the contamination remain in the two later versions. In the Prague text we find:

el cuerpo cara oriente
y la candela enla mano

In the *Cancionero* the king is made to die in León, a place nowhere mentioned in the accounts that we have seen of the death of Ferdinand IV; the *Crónica de veinte reyes* tells us how Ferdinand I was taken ill at Santa María de Manzano, after which he moved to León, where he attended religious services before he moved to Castillo de Cabezón where the death-bed scene presumably was supposed to have taken place. The mention of León in the Antwerp text can be fairly easily explained. The Cambridge version of this ballad is closely related to the *Romance de Fernando primero* printed in the *Cancionero de Amberes*; traces of this portion of the ballad remain in the two later versions of the ballad on the death of the Carvajales.

---

[1] *Cancionero de Amberes, ed. cit.,* p. xx.

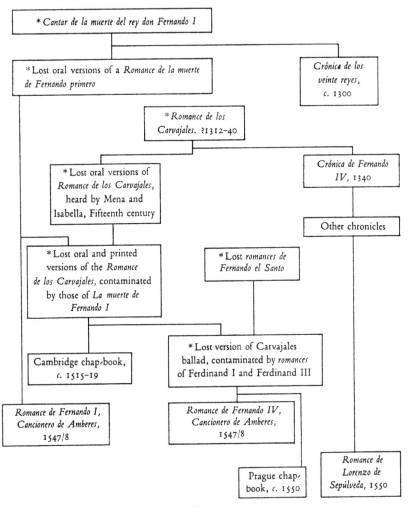

Fig. 1

Perhaps the following scheme for the history of the *romance* will have the assent of those interested in these questions:

1065. Death of Ferdinand I.

Before 1300. Minstrels sing of the scene at his death-bed.

1252. Death of Ferdinand III—Fernando el Santo.

After 1252. Minstrels sing of his acts of piety.

1312. Death of Ferdinand IV.

Before 1340. Songs sung about the summoning of Ferdinand IV, which continue during the 15th century (Juan de Mena, *c.* 1440; Isabel the Catholic, reigns 1479–1504).

*c.* 1517. Cambridge chap-book version of the ballad of the Carvajales, which incorporates a ballad derivative of the epic about the death of Ferdinand I.

1547/8. *Cancionero de Amberes.* It contains a version of the ballad of the Carvajales, contaminated by another about Ferdinand III's piety. It also contains a separate version of the *Romance de Fernando primero.*

?1550. Prague chap-book version of the ballad of the Carvajales, closely related to that mentioned above. Both versions bear traces of contamination from the *Romance de Fernando primero.*

The preceding very tentative stemma (Fig. 1) can account for most of the phenomena that I have outlined; it must not be considered definitive. It takes no account of the possibility that two versions of the ballad co-existed before 1547, only one of which contains an account of how the Almirante arrested the Carvajales. I have tried to depict the simplest explanation of the transmission of this *romance.*

## (v) *Otro romançe de Nuñez*

This is the only ballad in the Cambridge chap-book which can be proved to have been printed at an earlier date. It was printed in the *Cancionero general* of 1511. The chap-book version is corrupt in four lines; I therefore print here the early text with the abbreviations expanded:

*Otro [romance] de Nuñez*

Por vn camino muy solo
vn cauallero venia
muy cercado de tristeza
y solo de compañia
con temor le pregunte
con pesar me respondia
que vestidura tan triste
que por dolor la traya
dixome todo lloroso
que su mal no conoscia
quela passion que mostraua
no era la que padescia
que aquella vestia el cuerpo
la otra ellalma vestia
en su vista se conosce
que mal damores traya
conlos ojos lo mostraua
conla lengua lo encobria
contento de su penar

su mal por bien lo tenia
apartando se de mi
aqueste cantar dezia

El menor mal muestral gesto
quel dolor
no lo consient[e] el dolor

La prision ques consentida
por parte del coraçon
es prision que su passion
jamas no halla sallida
Por que la pena escondida
con dolor
publicalla es lo peor[1]

The Cambridge chap-book reads:

con pesar le respondia

la otra el alma vestia

con temor de su penar

aquesta cancion dezia

The misprints illustrate the fallibility of chap-book printers, even when they had a good printed text to follow. The poem was reprinted in the *Cancionero de Costantina* and in other reprints of the *Cancionero general*, in the *Cancionero de Amberes* and in the Prague chap-books.[2] There would be little point in quoting variants from these sources.

In this poem Núñez contrasts the outward appearance of grief with the inner sorrow which gave rise to it; his hero luxuriates exclusively in the inner sorrow. There are many contemporary parallels to this portrayal of love's willing martyrs; these verses, less effective than others by Garcisánchez de Badajoz or Juan del Encina, are not negligible. One wonders how this attempt at a refined analysis of feeling appealed to those who wanted to buy the stories of the escape of Don Gayferos or of the sad fate of the Carvajales and of King Ferdinand IV. Perhaps the poetry-readers of the early sixteenth century had catholic poetic tastes.

### (vi) *Romançe de la presa de Bugia*

The Spaniards captured Bugía (or Bougie) in 1510, and the city remained in their hands until 1555, when it was retaken from them by the Algerians. Zurita gives

[1] *Cancionero general* (Valencia, 1511), facsimile edition edited by A. Rodríguez-Moñino (Madrid, 1958), fol. cxxxviij[r].
[2] *Cancionero de Juan Fernández de Costantina*, ed. R. Foulché-Delbosc (Madrid, 1914), no. 193; *Cancionero de Amberes, ed. cit.*, fol. 214[r]; *Pliegos*, Praga, 1, no. XVI.

various details of the capture. The king was Abdurrahamel who, according to the Spaniards, usurped the throne, to which his nephew Muley Abdalla had a better claim. The Spanish fleet sailed from Ibiza on the eve of Epiphany, but contrary winds prevented their landing until the following day. Abdurrahamel was thus given the opportunity to line up his men on the mountain that overlooked the landing place; he had some horse and over 10,000 foot soldiers. After some fighting the Moorish king withdrew into the town, which the Spaniards captured after a three-hour battle, when many Moors were killed. Abdurrahamel and his men shamefully (*vilmente*) abandoned the city on the other side. His resistance in the country prevented its conquest, but the Spaniards continued to hold Bugía itself, where Muley Abdalla returned.

No other text of this ballad appears to exist. It can hardly be called traditional; it is a street ballad. Especially at the beginning it seems extremely prosaic:

> En vna parte del mundo
> que affrica se dezia
> caminando yo de priessa
> por negocios que tenia...
>
> Vi venir en medio dellos
> vn hombre de gran estima...

But as we read on the old ballad-theme of the grief of a king who has lost his kingdom, with phrases, even, from the minstrels' repertoire, makes us aware of a relation to older and better balladry:

> Agora fuesse yo muerto
> pues tal perdida perdia
> oy se pierden los mis reynos
> oy pierdo mi señoria
> oy pierdo la mi corona
> ya no soy quien ser solia...
>
> Este es el desdichado
> que rey era de Bugia
> este pierde oy su reyno
> que ya nada le valia...

King Abdurrahamel echoes Roderick the Goth, before the final lines emphasize the patriotic jingoism of the street singer. The singer, however, remembered the traditional ballads while he was composing his pastiche.

# CHAPTER VI

## Oral and Printers' Variants in Sixteenth-Century Texts of Spanish Ballads

THE statements about oral improvisation and set phrases in modern Yugoslav ballads, made originally by the late Milman Parry and developed by Mr Albert B. Lord,[1] have been taken into account recently by a few scholars in relation with Spanish ballads and medieval epics. Mr Lord's material consisted mostly of lengthy traditional poems, and their transmission was almost entirely oral, so that Spanish epics like the *Poema de Mío Cid*, the *Mocedades de Rodrigo* and the *Roncesvalles* fragment provide a suitable testing ground. Articles by Dr L. P. Harvey, Mr A. D. Deyermond and Miss R. H. Webber generally accept theories of improvisation for these poems.[2] Our ballads are much shorter poems, and the part played in their transmission by printed chap-books and anthologies introduces possible complications that Mr Lord had hardly to take into account. Before his interesting book appeared, Miss Webber applied Milman Parry's findings to Spanish ballads and found in them a similar use of set phrases.[3] She took as her basic text Wolf and Hofmann's *Primavera y flor*; she did not try to see whether different versions of *the same* ballad showed traces of improvisation. 'Formulistic diction' certainly occurs in these poems, but this is not to assume that Spanish sixteenth-century ballads were necessarily composed by improvisation at each performance. A period of improvisation may perhaps lie in the poems from which some of our ballads derived; she has not proved that ballads like those studied here were produced by improvisation.

The part played by printed *cancioneros*, *romanceros* and *pliegos sueltos* in their trans-

[1] Albert B. Lord, *The singer of tales* (Cambridge, Massachusetts, 1960).

[2] L. P. Harvey, 'The metrical irregularity of the *Cantar de Mío Cid*', *Bulletin of Hispanic Studies*, XL (1963), 137–43. A. D. Deyermond, 'The singer of tales and mediaeval Spanish epic', *ibid.* XLII (1965),

1–8. Ruth House Webber, 'The diction of the *Roncesvalles* fragment', *Homenaje a Rodríguez-Moñino* (Madrid, 1966), II, 311–21.

[3] Ruth House Webber, 'Formulistic diction in the Spanish ballad', *University of California Publications in Modern Philology*, XXXIV (1948–52), 175–277.

mission has not yet been assessed. Thanks to the recent republication of many of these texts by Sir Henry Thomas, Professor Rodríguez-Moñino and Don Carlos Romero de Lecea, the task seems more possible. We can now see how numerous the printed versions of such ballads were; some of them even continued to be reprinted until at least the second half of the nineteenth century.[1] Not till we have studied the kinds of variations that existed in different printed texts of the same Spanish ballads can we begin surely to test some of Mr Lord's findings. His work remains none the less extremely stimulating, but—as far as printed texts are concerned—much more learned donkey-work remains to be done before we can decide how the singers of 450 years ago used their set phrases and formulas.

Many scholars are unaware that in some places different methods of oral composition once flourished. I quote a few sentences from a recent, comparatively unnoticed work by Professor Kenneth H. Jackson:

From early sources other than the hero tales we learn that the [highly trained class of poets and sages called *filid*] were likewise trained in schools, where they were taught by a qualified *fili*. The course lasted from seven to twelve years; and they learned composition in the various metres, antiquarian and other traditions...[and] a very large number of the classic tales...Their songs were recited to the music of the harp. The bardic schools remained alive in Ireland until...the seventeenth century...The teacher taught metres and set subjects for composition, which was done by the pupils in their heads, lying on their beds in the dark; and then they recited their verses to him for corrections. The method of composition in Gaelic Scotland was very much the same, according to a description dating from the end of the seventeenth century. The poet shut himself indoors for a whole day, with his head covered with his plaid, while he composed a panegyric...Though the Irish poets were able to recite orally an immense amount of verse, including narrative verse, they did *not* do so by improvisation.[2]

Can we be sure that nothing of this sort ever happened in Spain?

We must suppose that any given text of an oral *romance* printed in a chap-book or in a longer *romancero* was a survival from a unique performance only which varied in different ways from thousands of other lost singings or recitations. No folk-singer sings a long song twice without altering it. Printers, by taking a single set of variants, established a definite poem which, as it was reprinted, must have tended to standardize what had hitherto been fluid. As printers generally preferred to set up from a printed text rather than from manuscript, later chap-book versions of *romances* often closely resemble earlier ones. The later printings of *Morayma*, of *Fonte frida* and of *Rosa fresca*,

[1] E.g. *Romance del conde Alarcos*. See E. M. Wilson, 'Samuel Pepys's Spanish chap-books', *Transactions of the Cambridge Bibliographical Society*, II, 4 (1957), 306–7.

[2] Kenneth Hurlstone Jackson, *The oldest Irish tradition: a window on the Iron Age*, The Rede Lecture (Cambridge, 1964).

all of which first appeared in the *Cancionero general* of 1511,[1] hardly differ at all from the text first printed. So that printed versions may—through their wide diffusion in the Peninsula and beyond it—have caused some reduction in the number of oral variants of some *romances*; singers may well have—for some years at least—come to rely more and more on these sheets as the sixteenth century advanced.

Printers, though, are men, not machines. The sixteenth-century printer or journeyman must from time to time have had before him a text of a ballad that he already knew by heart. And the version he knew must have differed in some respects from his copy text. When this happened he may possibly have set up variants from his own version because of his own personal preference for them. So oral variants may sometimes—perhaps often—have caused printers' variants in Burgos, Seville, Valladolid and other centres of ballad distribution. Now that we are beginning to have some knowledge of a larger number of sixteenth-century *pliegos de romances* we should try to see how much this may have happened. The task is not easy, but at least we can indicate some of the difficulties that lie in the explorer's path.

The *pliegos sueltos* or chap-books were intended principally for cheap popular sale, and probably there was little correction of them during the process of printing. There exists a possibility that there may have been, but the number of surviving *pliegos* probably does not include many duplicates. Any real duplicates should be closely examined to see whether this happened or not. Corrections if any exist, would affect our investigation. Readers will notice a number of obvious misprints in the facsimile text:

baldoninos (p. 75, column 2, line 23)

los manos (p. 78, column 2, line 23)

o que mal doliente haze (p. 79, column 1, line 8)

que ponga en cobre sus tierras (p. 80, column 2, line 24)

There is nothing unusual in such errors, and they often slipped past official correctors of more learned books. Nevertheless they are pretty glaring mistakes; one may suppose that no corrector was at work on this chap-book when it was printed at Burgos in 1515–19.

Probably there were no elaborate house rules with many chap-book printers at this time. But every journeyman would know that some spellings were old-fashioned, and on reprinting an earlier version he would tend to bring the spelling up to date. Some obvious instances of this practice are to be found in nos. ii, iii, iv in comparing our

[1] *Ed. cit.*, fols. cxxxv^v; cxxxiiij; cxxxij.

text with later versions (fablo > hablo, oyres > oyreys, etc.). But he might not invariably do so. Sometimes, if he were copying an obviously earlier work, he might possibly keep in his modern text some characteristic archaisms. On the whole, successive printers of popular *romances* tended to remove both archaisms and uncommon words; sixteenth-century printers of *El conde Alarcos* printed its first lines: 'Retrayda esta la infanta', later ones put 'Retirada está la infanta'.

The variants that we quoted above between the *romances* in the Cambridge copy and those in the Madrid and Prague *pliegos* from time to time illustrate this tendency. Changes such as: fablo > hablo, oyeres > oyreys, carcellero > carcelero, falla > halla, saliras > saldras, need not be oral variants; they probably represent changes made by printers to make the poems acceptable to a more recent public. Other changes, made in the direction of greater metrical regularity, may sometimes have a similar explanation. On the other hand we must remember, as Don Ramón has often pointed out, the metre of ballads (especially of those that bear a relation with the vanished epics) was often irregular in the earliest versions but tended towards more or less correct octosyllables as the years passed by. Any change in a poem, however small, may affect its merit. There is often some charm in an archaically incorrect line; but one need not regard the earliest printed version as necessarily superior to later ones, though perhaps usually this will be the case. A printer's alteration, however, might give a better rhythm or expression to a clumsy old line.

Occasionally, no doubt, two completely distinct versions of a given ballad were printed by different printers in different places. This may well have happened with our *Romance fecho ala muerte de don Pedro Caruajal y de don Alonso su hermano* and the Prague 'Valame nuestra señora'. Some lines are identical and others rather similar, but (even if we disregard the interpolations in both versions) the differences are such that they probably occurred before the ballads were printed and therefore were due almost entirely to oral tradition.

In most cases, though, where we find sixteenth-century ballad texts repeated there seems to be a more direct relation between them. Don Ramón described the *Cancionero de Amberes* text of the *Romance del rey don Fernando quarto* as a 'recuerdo tocado' of the Prague chap-book.[1] The *Marsín* ballad consists of exactly 114 lines in the Cambridge and Prague chap-books; the Gaiferos ballad is exactly sixty lines long in both the surviving versions. It seems most unlikely that different oral recensions of

---

[1] *Ed. cit.,* p. xxv.

any *romance* of over, say, forty or fifty octosyllables would often have such equivalences. Perhaps we can safely state that where two early printed versions of a longish *romance* are of equal length, then both descend either from a common source or the later from the earlier. But as the printers themselves could not have been isolated entirely from oral tradition, the variants between the different texts of the same ballad may sometimes, notwithstanding, be due to oral tradition as well as to more sophisticated corrections. In the two ballads already mentioned in this paragraph, the following variations seem *possibly* traditional:

> questa enlos puertos daspa (despaña) (p. 76, column 1, line 3)
>
> vase por vna calle abaxo (ayuso) (p. 77, column 2, line 11)
>
> no falla por do andar (botar) (p. 77, column 2, line 18)
>
> esperasses tu al lalua (al dia) (p. 77, column 2, line 29)
>
> ya estaua en libertad (la christiandad) (p. 78, column 2, line 30)

But it would be unwise to be too dogmatic. The first, third, fourth and fifth examples might have been altered merely to correct imperfect octosyllables.

The greatest immediate need in Spanish ballad-studies today is that of dating the unimprinted *pliegos sueltos* of the sixteenth century and of identifying their printers. The guesses of Salvá are not good enough. Huarte and Castañeda[1] made an excellent start, and the findings of Sir Henry Thomas are reliable for the ballads he reprinted. But the task needs to be continued; the chap-books of Prague, Madrid, Oporto and Paris all require the same thorough study. Comparisons of black-letter type, of woodblocks and ornaments in chap-books and in other books that bear dates would tell us the full history and the geographic distribution of many ballads and poems. Until such a study can be carried out exhaustively, we must indulge in guesses. And the quality of some of the poems is worth more than guesses.

The earliest glosses of *romances* known to me occur in the *Cancionero general* of 1511.[2] Some of these were reprinted in later chap-books, and many others appeared thereafter in the same format. The glossed *romance* perhaps raises special problems. A gloss could not be too long a poem. The poet who composed it would almost certainly choose a fragment from a longer poem or compress it to suit a particular purpose. In other words, he would touch up his original. The gloss was the work of

---

[1] Vicente Castañeda y Amalio Huarte, *Colección de pliegos sueltos, agora de nuevo sacados, recogidos, y anotados...* (Madrid, 1929); *Nueva colección de pliegos sueltos...* (Madrid, 1933).

[2] *El conde Claros* ('Pésame de vos el conde...'). *El conde* ('Mas ēbidia he de vos cõde...'), *Rosa fresca, Fonte frida, Morayma, Durandarte...*

some particular man called Soria, Pinar, Tapia or Quesada, who would adapt the original poem for reasons that seemed good to him. Don Ramón's ideas about how *romances* tended to grow shorter as the sixteenth century advanced probably remain true enough, but sometimes the abbreviation was not the work of the ballad-singer but of a lettered poet who did the job for reasons that had little to do with oral tradition, though he may have shared with the singer a feeling that shorter ballads were better than longer ones. The Prague chap-book's abbreviation of the *Romance de Amadís* is not a solitary case. Something similar may have happened with *La difunta aparecida* and with other traditional narratives.

A printer of *pliegos sueltos* is likely to have felt that he had to fill his four leaves or his customers might feel defrauded. (There are sometimes blank pages in surviving examples, but they are relatively uncommon.) He knew in advance how many lines of type were available to him. He would know how many lines of a given original or series of originals he ought to print. There may have been times when the work that lay before him was too long to be included on four leaves. He may, for instance, have had a *pliego* of another printer which was in type smaller than that he had available. In such circumstances he may have decided to omit certain lines from his original, and he would probably try to include what he thought were to him the most significant lines. I suggest that some sixteenth-century shortenings of ballads may possibly be caused by the necessities of the printing house. Perhaps the printer's position, like that of the poets who wrote glosses, was not really so very far from that of the folk-singer who could—at will—produce either a longer or a shorter version of a given ballad.

If we want to try to separate oral from printers' variants in two or more impressions of a sixteenth-century *romance*, we find that there are many common influences at work. Printer and singer were capable of introducing minor variants in transmission, in slowly modernizing and regularizing their received texts, in shortening what appeared to be prolix and in occasionally conflating different ballad texts. Major variants between printed versions may have been due to the knowledge of other versions by the printer himself or to a more literate sophistication by a corrector or by a *recopilador*. Sophisticated changes might also be produced by the poets who glossed *romances* or portions of *romances*. How far the printers tended to standardize what the singers continued to sing must remain conjectural, but in sixteenth-century Spain the widespread distribution of printed versions of ballads can hardly have failed to influence their oral transmission.

# CHAPTER VII

# *The Salamanca Chap-book*

THIS work is—from a literary point of view—disappointing. It is what appears to be a unique text of seventy-three ten-line stanzas. The anonymous author tells us that 'so titulo de disbarates [*sic*] algo dize delo que quiere: z vna cosa suenan algunas delas coplas: z otra entienden, de suerte que debaxo del sayal ay al'. It claims to be, then, a nonsense poem with a serious kernel. Seven hundred and thirty lines of nonsense are likely to defeat most readers, and the moralizing poetry of the early sixteenth century is often a bit tedious too. We have not exhumed a masterpiece.

Spanish nonsense poetry has been little studied, though the seventeenth-century *Coplas de trescientas cosas más* have received some attention.[1] During the Spanish golden age the *Disparates trobados por Juan del Enzina*, first published in 1496 in his *Cancionero*, became popular and remained famous.[2] The most serious study of the phenomenon was that of 'Marcel Gauthier' in the *Revue Hispanique* of 1915.[3] He listed various examples including poems by Jorge Manrique, Pedro Manuel de Urrea, Diego de la Llana, Gabriel de Saravia, Joaquín Romero de Cepeda, Francisco López de Úbeda and later writers.

The following list incorporates such nonsense poems as we have been able to find among Spanish sixteenth-century chap-books:

[1] R. Foulché-Delbosc, '*Coplas de Trescientas cosas más*', *Revue Hispanique*, IX (1902), 261–8; *ibid.* X (1903), 234–5. John M. Hill, 'Adiciones a las *Coplas de trescientas cosas más*', *ibid.* LXXII (1928), 527–9. E. M. Wilson, 'Samuel Pepys's Spanish chap-books, Part III', no. 63/56 (E), *Transactions of the Cambridge Bibliographical Society*, II, 4 (1957), 313. Antonio Rodríguez-Moñino, *Los cancionerillos de Munich* (Madrid, 1963), nos. 65–6, pp. 172–5. Maxime Chevalier and Robert Jammes, 'Supplément aux *Coplas de disparates*', *Mélanges offerts à Marcel Bataillon par les hispanistes français* (Bordeaux, 1962), 358–93.

[2] Quevedo referred to them in his *Visita de los chistes*, see Astrana Marín's edition of the *Obras en prosa* (Madrid, 1932), p. 181. Gonzalo Correas, in his *Vocabulario de refranes*, noted the phrase 'Disparates de Juan de la Encina' and added the comment: 'Escribió coplas de ellos con gracia, y acomódase a todos disparates' (Madrid, 1924, p. 162).

[3] 'De quelques jeux d'esprit. I. *Les Disparates*.' XXXVII, 385–45. 'Marcel Gauthier' was apparently one of the pseudonyms of R. Foulché-Delbosc.

Reprehension de vicios y estados en general. . .

[On leaf 4: Disparates.    En vnos montes espessos
cercados de clauellinas. . .]

British Museum. See *List of poetical chap-books*, no. 66.

Disparates cõtrarios de los de Iuan del enzina fechos por Aluaro de toro.

Bibliothèque Nationale, Paris. See *List of poetical chap-books*, no. 82.

Almoneda en disparates. Nueuamente hecha. Cantase al tono de las Gambetas.

[*Pliegos*, Madrid, III, no. CV. ?Gauthier, no. IX.]

Disparates muy graciosos. Ahora nueuamente conpuestos por Diego de la llana d[e]
la villa de Almenar. Y otros en carta a vna señora q̃ el seruia: suplicãdole le tẽga por
suyo. Y otros a vna borracha.

[*Pliegos*, Madrid, III, no. XVII. ?Gauthier, V.]

Disparates muy graciosos y de muchas suertes nueuamente hechos. Y vn aparato de
guerra que hizo Mõtoro. Y vnos fieros que haze vn rufian contra otro. [*Pliegos*,
Madrid, IV, no. CXXXVI. Similar text in British Museum: C.39.f.28.(4).]

Muchas maneras de coplas z villancicos con el juyzio de Juan del Enzina. British
Museum. See *List of poetical chap-books*, no. 30.

Disparates y almoneda trobados por Juan del enzina. E vn villancico.

[Antonio Rodríguez-Moñino, 'Los pliegos poéticos de The Hispanic Society of
America (siglo XVI)', *Hispanófila*, 1961, 13, 53–73, no. XI.]

There is no consistent metrical or stanza pattern in these poems. Some are in
octosyllabic couplets (*pareados*), some are *letrillas*, and Encina used a nine-line
rhyming stanza. The Cambridge chap-book poem is in stanzas of ten lines each.
The nature of the genre lies rather in the topsy-turvy subject-matter than in the metre.
As far as I am aware the three poems by Juan del Encina (*El almoneda, Los disparates*
and *El juyzio*) are the earliest Spanish examples of the genre. There were medieval
nonsense poems in France years before, called *fatrasies*, recently studied and edited by
Mr Lambert C. Porter.[1] Of these poems Dr Rickard has said: ' Actions are attributed
to incongruous agents, matter becomes animate, *extra naturam* characteristics are
freely bestowed, there is much far-fetched coming and going. . . much violent action,
much comic slaughter and not a little obscenity.'[2] Some of these characteristics can

---

[1] *La Fatrasie et le fatras: Essai sur la poésie irrationelle en France dans le Moyen Age* (Paris and
Geneva, 1960.)

[2] Peter Rickard in *French Studies*, XV (1961), 363.

be found in the Spanish poems too, except perhaps the obscenity and the violence. Encina made San Çorito ride on a pig, Jerusalem saddle a hack, a butterfly sell offal, Rome ride on horseback over the sea and have a battle fought for the sake of some watercress.

Our anonymous author seems to have used Encina's three poems to inspire him for his task:

| LINES | CAMBRIDGE TEXT | ENCINA'S 'JUYZIO' | LINES |
|---|---|---|---|
| | | Mas quiero como supiere | |
| | | declarar las profecias | |
| | | que dizen que en nuestros dias | |
| 10 | veran lo los que lo vieren | sera lo que dios quisiere: | |
| | | por que nadie desespere | |
| 106–10 | y enel año de secientos | hasta el año de quinientos | |
| | ya passado el de ochocientos | bivira quien no muriere | |
| | segun dizen los profetas | sera cierto lo que fuere | |
| | reboluer sean [sic] las veletas | por mas q̃ corrã los vientos. | 21–30 |
| | al combatir delos vientos | | |

| | | ENCINA'S 'DISPARATES' | |
|---|---|---|---|
| 128–9 | y esse valiente sanson | diziendo muera Sanson: | |
| | cantando kyrieleyson | y vino Kyrieleyson | 23–4 |
| 251–2 | Quien ganare ganara | Acordo remifasol | |
| | al jugar la vadalassa | a jugar la badalassa | 91–2 |
| 379–80 | τ son buenos los pertrechos | Zabulon y Netalin | |
| | picados en almodrote | vi venir en almodrote | 28–9 |
| 533–4 | hazersea vna procession | y una manada de perros | |
| | de gaçapos por vn teso | vi venir en procession | 149–50 |

| | | ENCINA'S 'ALMONEDA TROBADA' | |
|---|---|---|---|
| 10 | veran lo los que lo vieren | y unas nuevas profecias | |
| | | que dizen que en nuestros dias | |
| | | sera lo que dios quisiere | 25–7 |
| 370 | o çurran bien el valdres | y coraças de baldres | 79 |
| 379–80 | τ son buenos los pertrechos | y tres o cuatro tinajas | |
| | picados en almodrote | atestadas de almodrote | 125–6 |
| 613–14 | que heruetas las ortigas | y darles muchas hortigas | |
| | para tratar las sin guante | para que coman sin pan | 175–6 |

| LINES | CAMBRIDGE TEXT | ENCINA'S 'ALMONEDA TROBADA' | LINES |
|---|---|---|---|
| 633–4 | que lana la del herizo | dos albardas por colchones | |
| | para henchir almohadas | por cabeçales serones | |
| | | llenos de pluma de erizos | |
| | | Y dos savanas delgadas | |
| | | de sedas de puerco espin[1] | 61–5 |

In the Cambridge text the humour nearly always resembles that of Encina's *Juyzio...de lo mas cierto de toda la astrologia*. I quote one stanza from that poem:

En el tiempo que llegaren
a ser los dias mayores
seran las noches menores
quando mas ellas menguarẽ:
y los tiempos que passaren
passaran con tal vitoria
que los q̃ despues quedaren
duraran quanto duraren
por que dure su memoria. (109–17)

We have here the classic 'verdades de Pero Grullo'. The imitation is rather pallid:

Enel año venidero
quien barua quisiere hazer
la cabeça ha de boluer
ado quisiere al [*sic*] baruero
τ tambien el ballestero
que enel blanco quiere dar
ha siempre de procurar
de le herir enel medio
tan poco terna remedio
quien no pudiere escapar (201–10)

As in Encina much play is made with proper names, geographical and historical, introduced incongruously:

Los algarbes τ algezira
τ los caños de carmona
τ las fuerças de escalona
conel nicolao de lira
y el condado de altamira
y essa gran cibdad de gante
τ la villa de escalante
si anduuieren en debate
no passando xaque y mate
passara el sol adelante (171–80)

[1] All quotations from Encina are taken from the facsimile of the first edition of the *Cancionero* (first printed at Salamanca in 1496), published by the Spanish Academy in 1928.

From time to time the poet introduces some moralizing sentiments that make us see the point of his preliminary description: 'vna cosa suenan algunas delas coplas: τ otra entienden, de suerte que debaxo del sayal ay al'. There is a long warning against the wiles of women which begins in the 26th stanza and ends—more or less—in the 33rd. Other truisms later seem seriously intended:

> y los hechos hazañosos
> no se alcançan con dormir
> ni la fama con seguir [*sic*]
> la puedan los perezosos
> ni con estrados pomposos
> se alcanço el mas valer
> ni enlas virtudes crecer
> podra bien el que anda ocioso
> τ tambien el codicioso
> el costal podra romper
>
> E avn mas os quiero dezir
> que el que algo quiere tener
> del rabo dela muger
> le conuiene de salir
> prouecho τ honrra seguir
> τ no estar adormescido
> porque el paxaro enel nido
> despues que sabe volar
> por fuerça le a de dexar
> para ser bien mantenido (381–400)

The poem thus has two intentions: to amuse by stating the obvious and to state the obvious because it is seriously meant. This might—in the hands of a great writer—produce an interesting work of literature. But our imitative hack could not hope to bring it off. The nonsense is tedious; the positive recommendations are trite. Few will be surprised that this piece is known only in a single copy of a single edition.

# INDEX OF FIRST LINES

(Numbers refer to the list on pp. 13–30)

*Note.* The designation of form given in the text is indicated by the notes C (canción), D (deshecha), Dp (disparates), G (glosa), M (mote), P (perqué), R (romance), S (sola), V (villancico, villancete). Abbreviations are expanded and proper names capitalized. Words added in ( ) are variants.

A boca de sorna por yr encubierto, 39
A quien devo yo llamar (V), 1, 2
A quien miraran mis ojos, 74
Aborrir quiero Antonilla, 68
Abras me Madalenica, 40, 46, 47
Acojeme aca esta noche, 71
Al sereno esta el cordero, 17
Alça la boz el pregonero (V), 70
Alegrias alegrias, 64
Alterado el pensamiento (R), 78
Alto dios omnipotente, 14
Altos reyes poderosos, 16

Amadis el muy famoso (R), 5
Amara yo una señora (R), 78
Amor quien de tus plazeres (V), 9
Assentado esta Gayferos (R), 36–8
Ave, ave que bolaste, 64
Ave reyna gloriosa, 52
Ave rosa speciosa, 53
Averos de bastecer, 63
Ay Sierra Bermeja (D), 81

Bendito sea aquel dia, 76

Caminando por mis males (R), 24, 55, 60
Caminando sin plazer (R), 75
Carnal fuera carnal fuera, 27

Casamonte alegre por mal te vieron, 42
Catalina de mi querida, 72
Como en veros me perdi, 33
Con asaz temor prosigo, 51
Con pena y cuydado, continuo guerreo, 17
Con vuestro plazer, 69
Condestable muy amado, 63
Consolaos males esquivos (D), 60
Consuelo de los naçidos (G), 23
Coraçon procura vida (D), 78
Cuydado no me congoxes (V), 75, 78

Daca Mingo ravia en ti, [41], 69
Dama cogida en tu hato (V), 79
De la luna tengo quexa (R), 9
De la llena de los rios, 44
De Mantua salen apriessa (R), 50
De Mantua salio el marques (R), 50
De mas cortesanas, 71
De vida desamparado, 20
Demonos al alegria (V), 25
Descubrase el pensamiento (R), 60
Despues que el esforçado (R), 3
Despues quel rey don Rodrigo, 26
Dezi me vos pensamiento (R), 70, 78
Dezid amigo (hermano) soys flor, 20, 55
Dezid vida de mi vida (P), 31

# INDEX OF AUTHORS OF SUBORDINATE WORKS AND OF EDITORS, ETC.

(Numbers refer to the list on pp. 13–30)

## SELECT INDEX OF
## TITLES OF SUBORDINATE WORKS

(Numbers refer to the list on pp. 13–30)

# Romançe de Amadis

(c. 1515–19)

# ¶ Romançe de amadis y oriana y

otro del rey Malsin: con otro del infante gayferos: τ otro q̃ dize.En jaen esta el buen rey.con otros dos romançes.

Amadis el muy famoso
hijo del buen rey de gaula
que amores fueron los vr̃os
con la muy linda oriana
hija del rey lisuarte
señor dela gran bretaña
que jamas por pensamiento
nunca el vno al otro errara
si vna vez que fue desdicha
por la reyna briolanja
Oriana tenia celos
y cierto mal lo pensaua
mucho la queria amadis
mas era amor de hermana
vn enano de amadis
al reues esto tomaua
segun se querian los dos

el amor los conquistaua
supolo de aqueste enano
la princesa oriana
tanto enojo rescibio
quel coraçon le lloraua
Oriana con gran pena
vna carta le embiara
que se fuese do no lo viese
que jamas verlo pensaua
quando amadis la leyo
el color se le mudara
perdiera todo el sentido
muy grandes sospiros daua
apartose del camiño
vase por vna montaña
la qual era muy espessa
q̃ enella hõbre no habitaua

su escudero Gandalin
jamas nunca lo dexaua
con palabras amorosas
consolar se lo pensaua
Pues aquesto mi señor
quié tan grã mal os buscara
pero consolaos señor
que remedio se esperaua
andando por la espessura
al pie de vna sierra agra
hallaron vna gran fuente
que tenia muy buen agua
quando la vido amadis
cerca della se apeara
apeose gandalin
y el cauallo le tomara
quitoles ambos los frenos
y enel prado los echara
quando boluio a su señor
echado se lo hallara
llorando delos sus ojos
dela su boca hablaua
Oriana mi señora
ay quien de vos me apartara
alli fablo Gandalin
bien oyeres lo que fablara
consolaos el mi señor
no vos deys vida tan mala
fiad enel redentor
quel es el que remediaua
alli respondio amadis
que con gran tristeza estaua
es mi dolor atan fuerte

que remedio no esperaua
Gandalin de desuelado
adurmiose cabo el agua
quando lo vido el amadis
sotilmente se leuantara
z los frenos escondiera
en vna espessura mala
porque mas no lo siguiese
gandalin que bien lo amaua
vase vn valle adelante
avn hermitaño llegara
El hermitaño que lo vido
mucho se marauillara
que por tan aspera tierra
nadie por alli passaua
quando se junto conel
muy cortes le saludara
Como venis cauallero
por esta tierra tan agra
Señor trae me mi ventura
la qual fue muy desdichada
si te plaze el hermitaño
que yo contigo me vaya
Plazeme dixo señor
plazeme de buena gana
digades me vuestro nóbre
que os vala la madre santa
Poned me lo vos señor
segun el gesto lleuaua
puso le Beltenebros
que assi se le figuraua
que era hóbre muy fermoso
z gran tristeza lleuaua

fueronse ala peña pobre
donde su hermita estaua
alli estuuieron los dos
haziendo la vida amarga
Quando oriana se vio
sin aquel que tanto amaua
lloraua delos sus ojos
que jamas nunca cessaua
embiaua lo a buscar
por la tierra z por el agua
hallaralo vna donzella
que por la mar nauegaua
que lo quiso su ventura
que aquella peña arribara
donde alli se conoscieron
z amadis se consolara
La donzella le dio luego
carta de su enamorada
pues que era cõtra el el yerro
que perdon le demãdaua
le pedia por merced
que fuese donde ella estaua
grã plazer tomo amadis
que era cosa muy estraña
salen dela peña pobre
van se ala gran bretaña
llegaron ala cibdad
que bastida se llamaua
quedo alli beltenebros
la donzella se passara
compro armas y cauallo
luego su via tomara
seruialo vn escudero

que la donzella dexara
Huuo grandes auenturas
fasta do su amiga estaua
que vencio diez caualleros
vn infante hauiã en guarda
y mato a ffamon gomadã
z vn su hijo que lleuaua
que cada jayan de aquellos
de solo ver lo espãtaua
a aquel gran rey Lisuarte
muertos gelos embiaua
quando vino aquella noche
viose con su enamorada
el gran plazer delos dos
enel mundo se pensara.
Fin.

# Siguese vn ro-
mance del rey Malsin.

¶ Ya comiençan los franceses
con los moros pelear
z los moros eran tantos
no los dexan resollar
alli fablo baldouinos
bien oyereys lo que dira
Ay compadre don Beltran
mal nos va enesta batalla
mas de sed que no hambre
a dios quiero dar el alma
cansado traygo el cauallo
mas el braço del espada
roguemos a don roldan

que vna vez el cuerno tanga
oyr lo ha el emperador
questa enlos puertos daspa
que mas vale su socorro
que toda nuestra sonada
oydo lo ha don roldan
en las batallas do estaua
no me lo rogueys mis primos
que yo rogado me estaua
mas rogadlo a dõ renaldos
que ami no melo retrayga
ni melo retrayga en villa
ni melo retrayga en francia
ni en cortes del emperador
estando comiendo ala tabla
que mas querria ser muerto
que suffrir tal sobaruada
oydo lo ha don renaldo
quen las batallas andaua
Començara a dezir
estas palabras hablaua
O mal ouiessen franceses
de francia la natural
por tã pocos moros como est◆
el cuerno mandã tocar ( os
que si me toman los corajes
que me solian tomar
por estos z otros tantos
no me dare solo vn pan
Ya le toman los corajes
que le solian tomar
assi se entra por los moros
como segador por pan

assi derriba cabeças
como peras dun peral
por ronces valles arriba
los moros huyendo van
Alli salio vn moro perro
q̃n mal ora lo pario su madre
alcaria moros alcaria
si mala rauia vos mate
que soys ciento para vno
ysles huyendo delante
o mal aya el rey malsin
que sueldo os manda dar
mal aya la reyna mora
que vos lo manda pagar
mal ayays vosotros moros
que las venis a ganar
de questo oyeron los moros
avn ellos boluido han
y a bueltas z rebueltas
los franceses huyendo van
a tambien selos esfuerça
esse arçobispo Turpin
buelta buelta los franceses
con coraçon ala lid
mas vale morir con honrra
que con deshonrra viuir
Ya boluian los franceses
con coraçon ala lid
tantos matan delos moros
que no se puede dezir
Por ronces valles arriba
huyendo va el rey malsin
cauallero en vna zebra

no por mengua de rocin
la sangre que del salia
las yeruas haze teñir
las vozes que yua dando
al cielo quieren subir
reniego de ti mahoma
y avn de quanto hize en ti
hize te el cuerpo de plata
pies y manos de marfil
z por mas te hôrrar mahoma
la cabeça de oro te hize
sesenta mill cavalleros
offrecillos yo a ti
mi muger abrayma mora
offreciote treynta mil
mi hija mata leona
offreciote quinze mill
de todos estos mahoma
tan solo me veo aqui
y avn mi braço derecho
mahoma no lo traygo aqui
cortomelo el encantado
esse roldan paladin
que si encantado no fuera
no se me fuera el assi
mas yo me vo para roma
que christiano quiero morir
esse sera mi padrino
esse roldan paladin
esse me bautizara
esse arçobispo Turpin
mas perdoname mahoma
que con cuyta telo dixe

que yr me quiero a roma
curar quiero yo de mi.
Fin.
¶ Romance de gayferos.

Media noche era passada
y otra media por passar
quādo el infante gayferos
salio de cautiuidad
muerto dexa el carcellero
y quantos conel estan
vase por vna calle abaxo
como hombre mundanal
hablando en algarauia
como aquel que la bien sabe
yua se para la puerta
la puerta dela ciudad
halla las puertas cerradas
no falla por do andar
desque se vido perdido
empeçara de llamar
abras me la puerta el moço
si ala te guarde de mal
mensajero soy del rey
cartas le lleuo de mensaje
alli fablara el moço
bien oyres lo que dira
si eres mensajero amigo
cartas lleuas de mensaje
esperasses tu al lalua
con los otros saliras
De questo oyera gayferos
bien oyeres lo que dira

abras me la puerta el moro
si ala te guarde de mal
darte he tres pesantes de oro
que aqui no traya mas
oydo lo ha vna morica
que en altas torres esta
dizele desta manera
y empeçole de hablar
toma los pesantes moro
que menester te seran
la muger tenias moça
hijos chicos de criar
de que esto oyo el moro
rezio se fue a leuantar
las puertas questan cerradas
abriolas de par en par
acordose le a Gayferos
de vna espada que trae
la cabeça delos hombros
deribado se la ha
muerto cayo el moro
enel suelo muerto cae
de que esto vio la morica
empeço de gritos dar
ella los daua tan grandes
que al cielo quieren llegar
Abrasmonte abrasmonte
el señor deste lugar
qndo acuerdā por gayferos
ya estaua en libertad.
ffin.

Romāce fecho ala muer
te de dō Pedro caruajal
y de dō alōso su hermāo.

¶ En jaen esta el buen rey
esse buen rey don fernando
en jaen tuuo la pascua
y en martos el cabo daño
z vase para alcaudete
esse castillo nombrado
los pies tiene enel estribo
que no ha descaualgado
quando le dauan querella
daquesos dos hijos dalgo
de don pedro caruajal
z don alonso su hermano
que le robauan la tierra
y le corrian el campo
que le fuerçan las donzellas
a tuerto z a sin guisado
manda los prender el rey
z poner a buen recaudo
mandales cortar los pies
mandales cortar los manos
mandaualos despeñar
de aquessa peña de martos
o dela sierra de ayllo
porque caygan de mas alto
alli fablo el menor dellos
que era mas acostumbrado
emplazamos te el buen rey
para ante el rey delo alto
que de oy en treynta dias

que tu ayas de yr al plazo
oy cũples los veynte z nueue
de mañana has dir al plazo
ellos en aquesto estando
estas palabzas hablando
dio al rey vna maletia
quasi dolor de costado
o que mal doliente haze
esse buen rey don fernando
los pies tiene cara oziente
y la candela enla mano
a sus fijos todos quatro
a su cabecera tiene
z los tres eran ligitimos
el otro era bastardo
esse que bastardo era
quedaua mejor libzado
arçobispo de toledo
y enlas españas pzimado
si yo no muriera fijo
yo os llegara a padze santo
mas cõla renta ꝗ os queda
bien podzeys hijo alcançallo
z acabada esta razon
el alma a dios hauia dado
asi murio este buen rey
por la sententia ꝗ auia dado.
Fin.

## Otro romançe

de Muñez.

Poz vn camino muy solo
vn cauallero venia

muy cercado de tristeza
z solo de compañia
con temoz le pzegunte
con pesar le respondia
que vestidura tan triste
que poz dolor la traya
dixome todo lloroso
que su mal no conoscia
que la passion que mostraua
no era la que padescia
que aquella vestia el cuerpo
la otra el alma vestia
en su vista se conosce
que mal de amozes traya
con los ojos lo mostraua
con la lengua lo encobzia
con temoz de su penar
su mal poz bien lo tenia
apartando se de mi
aquesta cancion dezia.

### Desecha.

El menoz mal muestra el ges
quel mayor    (sto,
no lo consiente el dolor

La pzisió ques consentida
poz parte del coraçon
es pzision que su passion
jamas no halla salida
pozque la pena escondida
con dolor
poblicalla es lo peoz.
Fin.

# Romançe dela pre
sa de Bugia.

¶ En vna parte del mundo
que affrica se dezia
caminando yo de priessa
por negocios que tenia
yendo para vna ciudad
la qual se llamaua Bugia
vi que por toda su tierra
huya gran morería
de judios τ paganos
que esto era marauilla
los gritos que yuan dando
la tierra temblar hazía
Vi venir en medio dellos
vn hombre de gran estima
de su barua se messaua
que arrancar se la querría
lloraua delos sus ojos
dela su boca dezia
Agora fuesse yo muerto
pues tal perdida perdia
oy se pierden los mis reynos
oy pierdo mi señoria
oy pierdo la mi corona
ya no soy quien ser solia
Con estas palabras tales
asi mismo mal dezia
Allegueme a vn suyo
que mas a su costado yua
dixele dezid hermano
como vays tan de huyda
quien es esse cauallero

que assi maldize su vida
con lagrimas de sus ojos
estas palabras dezia
Este es el desdichado
que rey era de Bugia
este pierde oy su reyno
que ya nada le valia
pues que pierde la cabeça
de su reyno y señoria
Ha sela ganado el rey
de aragon τ de castilla
ha le tomado el tesoro
que enla ciudad tenia
y mucha buena hazienda
de morisma y judería
ha la ganado en qtro horas
ques vna gran marauilla
Por esso va tan huyendo
a buscar mas morería
para darle algun socorro
por ver si la cobraria
mas ya le he dado consejo
deso que se me entendia
q ponga en cobre sus tierras
essas pocas que tenia
quen ser vencido de tal rey
honrra grande le sería
Y dexe estar el socorro
que nada no le valdria
que a resistir a españa
no basta la beruería
ni todo el poder del turco
con toda su morería.

Fin.

[ 80 ]

# Juyzio hallado y trobado

(*c.* 1510)

# Juyzio hallado y trobado para emienda

de nueſtras vidas delas coſas que en nueſtros dias hã de acon
tecer ſacado por los curſos del cielo ꞇ planetas ꞇ eſperiencias ꝺ
las coſas que cada dia veemos. ꞏ Es la orden tal de eſta obra:
ꞇ proceder que ſo titulo de diſbarates algo dize delo que quiere:
ꞇ vna coſa ſuenan algunas delas coplas; ꞇotra entiendẽ. de
ſuerte que debaxo del ſayal ay al.

ꞏ Dela llena delos rios
cõuiene luego hablar
porque ſe han de leuantar
conlos yelos ꞇ los frios
tanto que no ſe dezir os
creſceran quanto creſcieren
correran quanto corrieren
para ariba o para abaxo
ꞇ ſi mi dezir deſſaxo
veran lo los que lo vieren

ꞏ E los peces coleando
del eſpanto que ternan
por las aguas andaran
como ſiempre fue nadando
andaran tanbien buſcando
lo que ſuelen por comer
no les faltara el beuer
ſi el agua no ſe ſecare
ſi alguno fuera ſaltare
el ſe tornara a meter

ꞏ Los delos rios cercanos
miren bien eſte juyzio
que ſera muy gran indicio
ſi ſe lauaren las manos

ꞇ moſar ſean los deſuanos
quando el agua alla llegare
ꞇ ſi mas ſobrepujare
no ſe eſcuſara con maña
de quedar con mal eſpaña
quando el mundo ſe abraſare.

ꞏ Será tan grãdes creſciẽtes
qual nunca naſcidos vieron
que los que ya ſe murieron
no podran paſſar las puentes
ꞇ de eſpantadas las gentes
comeran ſi lo tuuieren
ꞇ los que ſon ſi viuieren
no creſciendo mas las aguas
acoger ſean alas fraguas
por no eſcapar ſi pudieren

ꞏ Maſos digo deſdeagora
las puentes de ſalamanca
ſi el agua no las arranca
quedaran do eſtan agora
ꞇ ſi viniere adeſora
eſte diluuio notado
quedara el mundo eſpantado
ſin coiher ſi no lo han gana

a

y sera cosa muy vana
el temoz enel finado

℃ Las moliendas seran tales
que guarde bien quiê tuuiere
que si el agua no viniere
a entrar poz las canales
cresceran doblados males
conla falta del moler
el que pudiere tener
algun poco de barina
quanto mas lo comiere ayna
menos terna que comer

℃ Las auenidas mas duelo
que si cubzen los molinos
nadaran lo ansarinos
sin llegar los pies al suelo
z caera gran desconsuelo
sobze todos poz entero
que roto el maquiladero
y el agua sobze el tejar
si dentro quisiere entrar
sera loco el molinero

℃ Y con estas nueuas malas
las aues no lameran
ni tan poco volaran
sin estendijar las alas
y el que quisiere armarlas
sobze las aguas bolando
dando gritos bozeando
entrara con osadia
a pie enxuto poz la ria

si no se fuere mojando

℃ E las ondas dela mar
daran tan grandes bzamidos
que los que no son nascidos
nolo podzan escuchar
z los mudos por hablar
baran que no oyan los sozdos
enflaquesceran los gozdos
si no comen de temoz
z con este tal doloz
no podzan volar los tozdos

℃ Seran tantos terremotos
z de tanta foztaleza
que donde ouiere franqueza
bien podzan pascer los cotos
los que estuuieren remotos
de donde esto acontesciere
si en sus tierras no se oyere
dozmiran a buen sosiego
y el que entonce fuere ciego
alegrar se ha si lo viere

℃ Caeran muchos edificios
si no se pueden tener
cozreran se los officios
buscaran se artificios
para ganar de comer
y enel año de secientos
ya passado el de ochocientos
segun dizen los pzofetas
reboluer sean las veletas
al combatir delos vientos

Las peñas se batiran
si saltan de su lugar
ala fuerça del tronar
quiça algunas se caeran
arboles se arrancaran
mouidos los quatro vientos
faltaran muchos cimientos
cibdades villas lugares
hundir se han los alixares
si quiebran los fundamentos

Si quebrantare vna nao
de coz vna cigarra
no podra passar la barra
para venir a biluao
leuantar se ha menelao
y esse cipion africano
julio cesar el romano
y esse valiente sanson
cantando kyrieleyson
por el grande karlos magno

La muleta es peligrosa
si primero no se tresna
z peor traer de alesna
el gallo conla raposa
z la palabra engañosa
dela hembra para el ruyn
que segun dize merlin
vee se ala caualgadura
chapear la herradura
z ala muger el chapin

Quãdo elfuego esta encèdido

z con mas fuerça calesce
alas vezes acontesce
despues de hauer bien beuido
quedarse hombre adormecido
z avn al tiempo del baylar
si lo quereys bien mirar
da el villano çapateta
z anda hombre ala ruyneta
quando se vea mal tratar

No auran gana de comer
los perros despues de hartos
ni en galicia los lagartos
despues de muertos beuer
ni los niños aprender
antes que sepan hablar
z acabando de cortar
la enpeña el çapatero
antojar sele ha del cuero
conlos dientes de tirar

Enel mes de abril siguiente
seys z cinco haran onze
o en algun mes delos doze
avn que pese al concurriente
nascera el sol en oriente
z si por desdicha vierdes
en mayo los campos verdes
adelante el mes de julio
segun que lo dize el tulio
biuireys si no murieredes

Los algarbes z algezira
z los caños de carmona

z las fuerças de escalona
conel nicolao de lira
y el condado de altamira
y essa gran cibdad de gante
z la villa de escalante
si anduuieren en debate
no passando xaque y mate
passara el sol adelante

℃Leuantar sea vn torbellino
enel juego delas tablas
z son malas muchas hablas
segun dize el augustino
z santo thomas de aquino
z caeran dentro vn escriño
enla riuera de miño
si se quiebran las alcuças
quatrocientas mill lechuças
y espantaran a treuiño

℃Si vinieren de brauante
las olandas en babul
tornar sea el cielo azul
en tierra del almirante
nada desto no vos espante
que dentro en valladolid
se leuantara vna lid
de mosquitos enel ayre
ꝗ avn ꝗ lo ayays por ósgayre
despartira los el cid

℃Enel año venidero
quien barua quisiere hazer
la cabeça ha de boluer

sdo quisiere al baruero
z tambien el ballestero
que enel blanco quiere dar
ba siempre de procurar
de le herir enel medio
tan poco terna remedio
quien no pudiere escapar

℃Desto no tomen enojo
los que la codicia ciega
que despues de hecha la ciega
avn que seles salte el ojo
quedara seco el rastrojo,
y despues del pan cogido
z los paxaros en nido
ya passadas las vendimias
no ternan rabo las ximias
esto tened por creydo

℃E puesto el pan enel silo
segun muchos acostumbran
si las candelas alumbran
sera porque arde el pauilo
pero si quebranta el hilo
al que mucho anda enbeuido
quando mas le trae torcido
enel tiempo del vrdir
es peligroso el morir
o sera saluo o perdido

℃E quien quisiere comprar
enel monte alguna leña
acostumbrase en cerdeña
que el ꝗ compra ha de pagar

no me puedo remediar
con pedrica τ bien te quiero
que ni libros el librero
ni el trapero dara paño.
segun que se dize ogaño
si noles lleuan dinero

℃Andaras en mi seruicio
mas busca quien te mantenga
antes que quaresma venga
mas vale tomar officio
que seruir tal benefico
que en mi tierra sea sonado
que si nieua hara nublado
y enel val de san vincente
y de roma a benauente
conel ruyn passan el vado

℃Quien ganare ganara
al jugar la vadalassa
tambien se dize en mi casa
que ningun sonido hara
la nieue quando caera
porque suena en gascoña
que lança mucha ponçoña
el mirar dela muger
τ su traje y reboluer
es reclamo y enpoçoña

℃Halagan conlas orejas
y trepejan conla cola
no estaran vna ora sola
sin se componer las cejas
τ tal darle enlas cernejas

τ con tantos ademanes
enla muestra maçapanes
enla boca traen la miel
enel coraçon la hiel
enel morder alacranes

℃No cure del amor dellas
quien quiere estar sin passiões
que muestran sus afficiones
quando veen que fuys dellas
si seguis τ andays tras ellas
daros han mill cantonadas
borregas desuariadas
balan quando las dexays
huyen quando las amays
todas andan falseadas

℃Ellas quieren las ameys
penan si las oluidays
quieren que les descubrays
el amor que les teneys
no quieren que conoscays
aficion quando os la tienen
de tal suerte se mantienen
τ os quieren señorear
que si se veen os amar
en si mesmas lo retienen

℃Hazen lo con cautela
por os traer sojuzgado
que si os veys no ser amado
es matar se os la candela
açorado puesto en vela
no podeys assosegar
a iij

[ 87 ]

desuelando os en pensar
si como amays soys mirado
si soys por dicha oluidado
vos no podiendo oluidar

℃ Siempre juegan de reues
la suya puesta enel hito
τ vos cuytado maldito
sin valeros padesces
andays mozis reboluies
porque crean las amays
τ ellas quanto mas andays
trasportados en su amor
por os doblar el dolor
dizen por demas andays

℃ Si quereys mirar vereys
enellas vn gran ardid
que puestos mas enla lid
desque veen que no podeys
consejan las oluideys
saben vuestra perdicion
conocen vuestra presion
que no podeys oluidarlas
que no podeys no amarlas
dizen perded affficion

℃ Como la sombra se tratan
que huye si la seguis
sigue si vos rehuys
si las amays se leuantan
si las dexays os leuantan
que soys de paño frances
o que de ruyn lo hazes

o que soys frio o couarde
o no como dezis arde
el amor que las tenes

℃ La condicion del villano
que si vee os le humillays
ȷntos mas ruegos le hagays
se os tornara mas vfano
pero si le days de mano
traerles tras vos rendido
dizen que es amanescido
salido el sol en milan
τ avn en tierra del soldan
esto mesmo a acontescido

Mas os digo dome a dios
no os lo digo por demas
que enel quinientos y dos
cadavno querra mas
para si que para vos
veldo vos ni coraçon
que avn que esta cerca el jubõ
mas cerca esta la camisa
siempre biua τ altamisa
desconciertan en nacion

℃ E sin falta veres al
por hazer algun concierto
que el que vela esta despierto
τ de aqui otro mayor mal
que es el mundo interesal
del mayor hasta el menor
del menor hasta el mayor
del mas baxo hasta elmas alto

꙳ el mas alto es el mas falto
꙳ el que mas tiene el peoz

Delos grandes no hago cuēta
mas que no les demandeys
poz amigos los terneys
no se si enesto consienta
en dezir saben de cuenta
mejoz que vestir arnes
yo callo vos que dires
es assi como yo digo
o reuenden bien el trigo
o çurran bien el valozes

¶Calla mucho en oza mala
no pōgais lēgua enlos grādes
que de santiago hasta flādes
el blason tienen poz gala
quiça pisareys la pala
꙳ os mozdera enel cogote
꙳ alos niños con açote
les hazen andar derechos
꙳ son buenos los pertrechos
picados en almodzote

¶y los hechos hazañosos
no se alcançan con dozmir
ni la fama con seguir
la puedan los perezosos
ni con estrados pomposos
se alcanço el mas valer
ni enlas virtudes crecer
podza bien el que anda ocioso
꙳ tambien el codicioso

el costal podza romper

¶E avn mas os quiero dezir
que el que algo quiere tener
del rabo dela muger
le conuiene de salir
prouecho ꙳ honrra seguir
꙳ no estar adozmescido
porque el paxaro enel nido
despues que sabe volar
poz fuerça le a de dexar
para ser bien mantenido

¶Eneste mes en que estamos
primero medio o postrero
demostrara se vn letrero
enlos ayres que leamos
a dezir que nos vayamos
alo mas raso a esconder
que del cielo ha de llouer
algun poco si añublare
꙳ si de aquesto faltare
no cureys mas de entender

¶Enel sobzedicho mes
quasi en fin para salir
es cosa de no dezir
los q entonces lo veres
el cielo como lo vees
si no ay mudança alguna
estar sea do esta la luna
꙳ como estan las estrellas
casar sean /o no donzellas
no se mudara laguna

❡ Leuátar fea mucha efpuma
enlos montes perineos
τ quedaran los cozneos
en camas llenos de pluma
porque dizen quando abuma
es feñal que alli ay fuego
τ de aqui concluyo luego
que en tal lugar las eftopas
fe quemaran τ las ropas
fin encender mucho efplego

❡ Enefte mes ya nombrado
antes que entre el otro año
dizen que daran el paño
por lo que fuere comprado
no es razon que alo paffado
ninguno vaya a trabar
porque es cierto fin dudar
que fegun las mueftras fon
enel reyno de leon
todo ha feydo por burlar

❡ E fera vna gran jornada
defde oriente hafta occidente
τ la berruga enel diente
o. fera algo o no nada
τ vna legua bien tirada
del gallego hafta el folano
mayor que del pie ala mano
τ tanbien del dito al fato
alas vezes ay gran trato
fegun dize el ytaliano

❡ No penfeys va muy vfano

el pollo ni muy feguro
quando fe alça fobre el muro
enlas vñas del milano
ni lleuarfe mano amano
lobo rapofa y cordero
es por eftrecho fendero
leuantar al cielo el buelo
retoçar conel anzuelo
no es feguro al pez ni vero

❡ Peligrofo es contender
la perdiz conel açor
τ al ciego fin guiador
fobre la cerca el correr
τ podra acontefcer
el no fano eftar enfermo
y de genoua a palermo
yr frayles de dos en dos
y enel barco al fol de dios
defpues de quebrado el remo

❡ Dificultofo es de hallar
quien algo no toque en zayno
τ fi enefto defenvayno
la lengua en mi hablar
no os deueys marauillar
que por mas cierto os digo
deue fer puerta o poftigo
por do entran en feuilla
τ luego otra marauilla
que apena ay leal amigo

❡ E feran fegun mi fciencia
quemadas muchas enzinas
y muertas muchas gallinas

enla cibdad de florencia
τ avn aqui dentro en valécia
lo paſſado vaya atras
que jugar tres dos y as
`es gran daño a quien no ſabe
en ningun diſcreto cabe
ſi le engañan jugar mas .

℄ Ballo mas por eſcrituras
enel ſeycientos τ vno
que ſi no muere niguno
eſtar ſean las ſepulturas
tornar ſean las piedras duras
enel val de lorençana
τ ſi la oueja con gana
ala çarça va a paſcer
al tiempo del reboluer
bien podra dexar la lana.

℄ Tirte afuera jura a ſan
que es peligro tal entrada
que ſegun eſta enaziada
es por demas el afan
mas vale comer del pan
que fayſanes quien quiſiere
que ſi el ſol eſcureſciere
el dia de nauidad
lo dicho terna verdad
ſi vieredes que aconteciere

℄ Otra ſeñal eſpantoſa
ſe moſtrara eneſte valle
que ſera lançado vn dalle
de mano de vna rapoſa

el coraçon no repoſa
del que quiere mal bazer
que aprouecha bien querer
donde eſta cierta la yerua
dizen que aprieta la xerua
no madura enel morder

℄ Eneſte mes de enero
quien riere terna gozo
quien ſacare agua del pozo
ſi la ſaca con harnero
terna vano el calauero
en jugar la perſeguera
bien pareſce verdadera
la cuña con ſu figura
mas no ſufrira natura
que atras buelua la ribera

℄ Por concordar mi proceſo
deſta prenoſticacion
bazer ſea vna proceſſion
de gaçapos por vn teſo
no es poſſible cobrar ſeſo
quien aſſi ſe vee mordido
que ala fin queda perdido
quien traſperdido ſe anda
de valencia baſta miranda
muchos males ſe ban ſeguido

℄ E ſi quiſiera tornar
a ſu demanda τ porfía
o ſera noche o de dia
o querra deſatinar
començar ſe ba a derramar

la niebla cerrada escura
τ mirando su hermosura
delas partes orientales
renouar sele an los males
nunca cobrara cordura

¶ Otra señal de espantar
nascera por los poblados
que delos que juegan dados
cada vno querra ganar
si no se puede apartar
alguno desta pelea
no sabe lo que dessea
que es vn vicio de tal suerte
que ala clara trae la muerte
τ de callada guerrea

¶ Mostrar sea enel alto polo
la diosa pallas y venus
el dios jupiter y febus
por seguir al dios apollo
τ si se hallaren solo
enlos campos de venecia
resuscitara lucrecia
y en borgoña el duque charles
τ de aqui podreys echarles
vna lança dentro en grecia

¶ Cosa que me sobre puja
es enlas mugeres vna
que no quebranta niguna
por do quebranta el aguja
τ si la moneda puja
enel reyno de toledo

alegrar sean los de olmedo
τ ado mas dinero ouiere
τ quien nada no tuuiere
quedar se ha lamiendo el dedo

¶ Quan dulces en su dezir
que desfracen quando quieren
como amagan como hyeren
quan feroces en reñir
que assomar que rehuyr
si vos veen de yerua tocado
que semblante alborotado
que fingen por os matar
estudian de vos desdeñar
quando os veen apassionado

¶ Los que quisieren cantar
pienso que abriran las bocas
τ la gente delas tocas
sabra con su trebejar
sin tijeras tresquilar
ar ar ar quan alto buelo
que da con hombre enel suelo
enla mano regaliz
enla lengua la lombriz
y de secreto el anzuelo

¶ Será grandes marauillas
τ vn juego trauiesso tal
que alas vezes trata mal
la chueca las espenillas
y desnudas las rodillas
encima delos abrojos
no biuireys sin enojos

ni en plazeres sin esto:bo
τ tambien soplando el poluo
a vezes salta a los ojos

℄Quien se viere malandante
no biuira sin fatigas
que heruetas las ortigas
para tratar las sin guante
quien no mirare adelante
podra dar consigo a tras
quien bien tiene y busca mas
puede se quedar sin nada
codicia es desordenada
querer salir de compas

℄Guarda guarda q̃ rescuña
el gato jura a sanhedro
que segun dize san pedro
es el diablo la guarduña
τ avn peligroso de viña
el osso brauo montero
dix que bonito romero
halaguero quan humano
que os halaga con la mano
τ da con el majadero

℄Nunca las vi bien medradas
las viñas con el granizo
que lana la del herizo
para benchir almohadas
las riquezas muy guardadas
daño son de su señor
τ zun zun al derredor
muerde el abeja y ampolla

τ quando mas hierbe la olla
el soplo mata el herbor

℄No valdra tanto el estaño
como el oro en portugal
ni el picote ni sayal
como grana τ fino paño
que muestra la del castaño
en el tiempo del cerner
quan agradable de ver
mas si llegays a la fruta
despues de seca y enxuta
la mano os podra morder

℄Los que gran fama desean
no duermen en guerrear
ni el ladron que va a hurtar
aguarda quando le vean
ni al que assaetean
le reposa el coraçon
ni tiene sana intencion
el perro quando regaña
segun se suene en españa
reniego tal afficion

℄Mira quan amodorrido
anda anton por el collado
cata que esta espeluncado
algo deue hauer perdido
digo os que dara tronido
quando cayere algun rayo
en solo vn punto desmayo
que me mata y desatina
que es mala fruta el andrina

z de buen parlar el jayo

¶Si pleytos cessan de andar
enessa chancilleria
quien mas tiene mas querria
mas al tiempo del dexar
es trabajo se apartar
a quien quiera delo que ama
el cuerpo tiene enla cama
y enel arca el pensamiento
enel coraçon tormento
mortal dolor enel alma

¶No digo por espantar
lo que snena en paladinas
que la zorra z las gallinas
nunca bien sean de tratar
z de mucho se parar
ala ventana la hermosa
enla mar que es reboltosa
la naue pierde la vela
z al fuego dela candela
las alas la mariposa

¶Quien las estrellas côtare
mira bien sepa de cuenta
que con dos vezes cincuenta
ciento hara sino pensare
z si por dicha tardare
en venir la nauidad
caera cierto de verdad
segun nuestras profecias
ante año nueuo ocho dias
digo os lo esto en puridad

¶Si se tornare amarillo
por dicha el resalgar
es forçado que han de dar
los relojes con martillo
z vestir sean de pardillo
los pardales con pedrisco
z guardaos del basilisco
z del son que es bondombon
porque donde echan carbon
siempre quedara algun cisco

¶Y sera otra marauilla
desde francia a portugal
que quien fuere a madrigal
z partir de alli a seuilla
bien se podra yr sin silla
si de pie ha de caminar
z quien se pone a esperar
los concejos a oxeo
tosca complira el desseo
al tiempo del desarmar

¶Si en tiempo delas eladas
juntos se acostaren tres
teniendo fuera los pies
z las cabeças colgadas
no las ternan leuantadas
porque enlas partes d europa
si el de en medio esta sin ropa
mal sudaran los del cabo
z con este fin acabo
la mano puesta enla copa
Fin.